Eugenio's New Neighbours

ABOUT THE AUTHOR

Margaret Gimson was born in Hong Kong and educated in England, with a year in France. In August 1939 she went to join her parents in Zanzibar, and on her father's retirement, she went with her parents to South Africa, and worked for several years as a nurse. In 1943, she returned to England, married and brought up a family in Leicester, studied French at Leicester University, and then worked as a Home Teacher until she and her husband went to Spain.

Eugenio's New Neighbours In Spanish Galicia

by

Margaret Gimson

Sunset Books

Copyright © Margaret Gimson 2008
First published in 2008 by Sunset Books
3 Daniells Close, Lymington, Hants, SO41 3PQ

Distributed by Gardners Books, 1 Whittle Drive, Eastbourne, East Sussex,
BN23 6QH
Tel: +44(0)1323 521555 | Fax: +44(0)1323 521666

British Library Cataloguing in Publication Data
A catalogue record for this book is available from the British Library.

ISBN 978-0-9556104-0-0

Typeset by Amolibros, Milverton, Somerset
This book production has been managed by Amolibros
Printed and bound by T J International Ltd, Padstow, Cornwall, UK

Contents

Antonio López Lillo, *well-known botanist*

From an article in *Zona Verde*, the journal of the Spanish Association of Parks and Public Gardens. 1992 (Translated)

"I have to say that seeing such a big collection (of plants) surprised me, not only for their number but for the rarity of most of the species. It was much more than 1 had imagined, and I thought that I was seeing the best private botanic garden in Spain..."

From a letter dated 5.10.2003. (Translated)

"It seems to us to be a very good idea to write this book, because we believe that it is necessary that the work that you and Robert did should be known. This should become history, as we think that history is made up of little histories like this one."

From a letter from *Patrick Bowe*, B ARCH, MRIAL, Architect and garden designer. 24.05.1987:

"I am writing to thank you very much for receiving the group of Fellows of the Royal Horticultural Society in your garden in March. It was undoubtedly the highlight of our tour and one of the highlights of my garden visiting in Europe over many years. "

Charles Puddle, MBE, VMH, until his retirement Head Gardener at Bodnant gardens, North Wales:

"Anyone who had the great pleasure of visiting La Saleta will have happy memories of the great friendship shown to them by Robert and Margaret. Not only was his friendly and helpful nature extended to visitors but to the local community in which they played a full part in organising local events."

List of Illustrations

The garden is featured in *The English Garden Abroad* by Charles Quest-Ritson, (1992) and *The Gardens of Spain*, photographs by Michael George and text by Consuelo Correcher, (1993)

Acknowledgements

Passage from *The Spanish Labyrinth* by Gerald Brenan reproduced by permission of the Author's Estate c/o Margaret Hanbury, 27 Walcot Square, London SE11 4UB. All rights reserved.

Cover photography: with kind permission of Señora María Gorbeña, from Santander, who was the photographer for a magazine called *Nuevo Estilo* who visited and did a feature on the La Saleta garden in 1998.

Preface

Margaret Gimson's Memories of Galicia

The Gimsons were a typical English family – unlike the usual stereotype – open, cultivated, not at all formal, comfortably off, and with a passion for plants, passed on to the rest of the family by its head, Robert. That they established themselves in Meis, Galicia, where they lived for more than twenty years, was because of the mild and damp climate of the region, which enabled them to create a most interesting botanical garden, and also because of the character of the country people, suspicious but generous, who accepted the Gimsons, "the English", into their world as if they were an integral part of it.

Doña Margarita, as they called her, is a woman of much personal sympathy, with an open mind and great intellectual curiosity, which must have something to do with having been born in Hong Kong and having lived in South Africa. I first met her when she visited the Provincial Historical Archives of Pontevedra, trying to find out the history of the small *pazo* – manor house – in the property they had bought. *The pazo* brought them into contact with the last remaining Galician aristocracy and the bourgeoisie, owners of similar properties.

Now, since Robert's death and Margaret's return to England and the scattering of their young around the world, our friendship is nurtured by her annual visits which refresh our precious memories of an extraordinary period of which she was a witness. Her memoirs are a most interesting testimony of how was archaic and traditional Galicia, and of how its incorporation into the modern world has come about in huge steps, which we now observe with astonishment from our situation as twenty-first century townees.

Pedro López Gómez

Pedro López Gómez, member of the Faculty of State Archivists of Spain, was Director of the Provincial Historical Archives of Pontevedra, and subsequently Director of the Archives of Galicia in La Coruña, when the Gimsons lived in Spain. At the moment he is Professor of Libraries and Documentation in the Faculty of Humanities of the University of La Coruña.

Part One

New Adventure

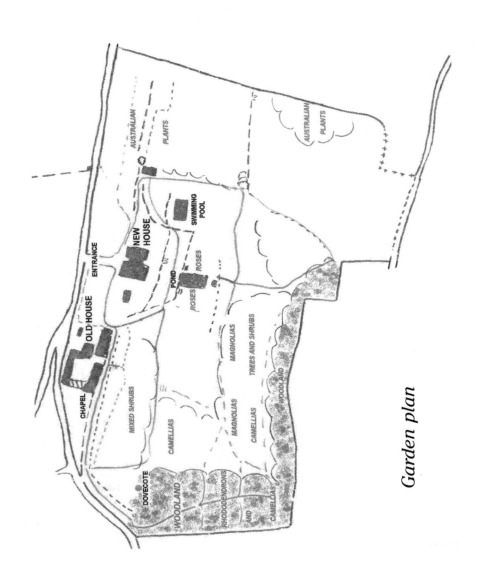

Garden plan

1

The arrival of strangers

"Acá xa sabemos o que hai ¿ alá que habrá?" (Gallego saying)
Here we know already what there is, and there –
what will there be?

"Is this the track?"

Robert turned the heavily laden car and trailer into pine and eucalyptus woods. We bumped along the track as he tried to avoid potholes and exposed rocks

Yes, round the next bend was the long stone wall. We paused a moment, holding our breath, to look down the slope with its tangle of weeds, golden fruit on an orange tree, gorse bushes in flower, and at the bottom, a belt of woodland. In the valley below were small emerald green fields and dark clumps of pines, and, beyond, the houses of a scattered village, grey stone houses with red-tiled roofs, their windows glinting in the afternoon sun. Behind the village was a line of low hills, and another and another.

We drove on, along the length of the wall and round the side of the old farm buildings and parked on the triangular expanse of rough grass in front of the gateway and grey stone chapel. Everything looked as beautiful as it had last summer, and now the old farm known as La Saleta was ours. How would this venture turn out?

It was February 1968 and we had come for a short holiday to Spain to look carefully at the property we had bought in Galicia, in the north-west of the country, for our retirement a few years later. This year, we knew there was no question of staying in the dilapidated old buildings, and had booked a hotel room in Pontevedra, the nearest town. But now there was daylight to spare and we could not bear to wait to see the place again.

We had been told to get the keys from Eugenio Mouriño, but to ask for *Eugenio del Pozo* (Eugenio of the Well). I went up a little path opposite in search of him.

I knocked on a gate, setting a guard dog barking and snarling, and a woman came out of the house. A round person in face and figure, she wore the usual peasant's black dress and black headscarf tied at the back of her neck and stout agricultural boots. She was Celina, Eugenio's wife she told me, and we must be those English people who had bought La Saleta. Eugenio had gone to a funeral, she said, and, fetching some huge iron keys from inside her house, she accompanied me down the footpath, questioning me as we walked. How many children had I? How old was I? I managed to reply forty-six and she exclaimed, "How young you look!" She was forty-eight, she told me. The question of age interests these country people intensely, and it is true that the women look much older than townswomen do, because working outdoors in all weathers wrinkles and darkens their skins. In those days Celina did a day's work on the farm that would have been far beyond my strength.

News travels fast in the country and our arrival must have been noticed. Eugenio came running to look after us. His place was with us, he explained. They showed us round every inch of the old buildings and helped us unpack car and trailer. As well as plants to start making a garden, we had brought some plates, cooking pots, buckets and a broom. We stacked it all in the least ruined of the outhouses to the astonishment of Eugenio and Celina. "Why not in the house?" they asked. We tried to explain that as the house would have to be repaired, we did not want to have to move everything out again. They were amazed and entertained at our medley of possessions. Presently Celina disappeared and Eugenio took us over every inch of the land, while we struggled to understand what he was telling us – plenty indeed – and examined every detail as he insisted we should do.

We owed a lot to Eugenio and Celina. At first we were dependent on their help for almost everything, and we had to trust them; and how lucky we were in having their help and friendship. Eugenio was a wiry little man, intelligent and thoughtful, but excitable – even fiery when aroused. He had an irrepressible sense of humour and considerable talent for mime, and sudden, anxious silences and moments of perplexity when some difficulty arose. He had been caretaker of the property in the absences of the previous owners and so naturally became caretaker for us, and Providence having dropped helpless and rich foreigners on him from the skies, he obviously took on responsibility for looking after us. Undoubtedly, there would be advantages to be obtained as a result. I do not believe that the genuine friendship he offered us right from the beginning was wholly disinterested, nor would he have pretended that it was, for the Galician countryman is very realistic, but I do not think that he cheated us or deceived us in any important matter. Sometimes though, he muddled us, or gave us the wrong advice.

This arrival, so momentous to us, was surely almost as momentous to Eugenio and Celina. Foreigners – English people – had bought La Saleta. A *señor* two metres high and a *señora* wearing a bright blue trouser suit! (The Galicians are a short stocky race, and in those days no females in the countryside wore trousers.) What would we be like? How would we behave? And, most urgent of all, how were we going to communicate?

Now, Eugenio insisted, we must go to their house to celebrate our arrival with a glass of his wine. His farm was small and well-kept, and his pride in it evident. Vines, all pruned and ready tied-up for the spring, maize field, potatoes, two cows and a horse, chickens and a pig, the animals being quartered on the ground floor of the house.

The living quarters were up an outside stone stairway. On the landing at the top was a modern wash basin but water had to be fetched from the well for us to wash our hands. Inside, the house was simple, clean and bare: a parlour furnished only with a cupboard, table and chairs, two little bedrooms and the kitchen. Here there was only room for a table, chairs and the iron wood-burning stove with a row of brown enamelled saucepans hanging above it. We were pressed to sit down and now we realised that Celina had vanished earlier in order to run home and prepare refreshments for us, slices of hard-boiled eggs and of chewy sausage, a dish of little pancakes with sugar, and large hunks of country bread. First we were served with their sharp white wine and urged to try the definitely sour red, while they asked question after question – about our children, what English food was like, why we liked Galicia, how pancakes are made, all of which was a great strain on our few words of Spanish.

"What are your names?" asked Eugenio.

"Gimson." There was a silence. Eugenio wrinkled his nose, perplexed.

"No, that isn't a name. What are your names?"

Robert took a piece of paper and wrote down: Robert Gimson, Margaret Gimson.

"Ah!" said Eugenio with great satisfaction. "Don Roberto and Doña Margarita, those are your names."

Two daughters and a son-in-law joined us. Introductions, explanations and more questions. It was dusk before we managed to leave, tired and bewildered, but what a warm welcome it had been! And with our new life we had acquired a new identity.

2

The beginning

"Dunha nos pequena nasce unha nogueira." (Gallego saying)
From a little nut grows a walnut tree.

Our delight in Galicia had begun eight years earlier, in 1960, when we visited Spain for the first time. Robert and I and our three children went to Galicia for a summer holiday with a car, a dictionary and a small phrase book. At that time there was a service of French Line boats to the West Indies, which called at Southampton and Vigo and returned three weeks later in the other direction. One hot August day we were disembarked at Vigo, at half past eight in the morning, and we found ourselves swept along into the customs building without any idea how to extricate the car from the quay below, where it had been dumped by the crane. The mechanics of Spanish officialdom are very difficult to understand, and it was a bedlam of noise and bustle. It was eleven o'clock when we finally managed to get the correct piece of paper and drive away into the city, hot and tired.

Once an independent kingdom, the region has kept its language and local culture and a strong sense of national identity, its people being as different from Spaniards in other parts of Spain as is the climate. It is a green land with hills covered with gorse and bracken and heather, and with deep river valleys and little streams. The basic rock is granite, and, in places, great grey boulders, smoothed by the wear and tear of centuries, lie about as if thrown down at random by some giant. In other places the rain has washed away the soil leaving jagged rocks, the exposed skeleton of the land. Along the deeply indented coast are sheltered bays and rocky headlands, beaches and sand dunes.

That first holiday we were enchanted by the beauty of this far corner of Europe. The small hotel we stayed in made no special effort to cater for foreigners, but the staff exercised much patience in trying to understand our requests, and disentangle our difficulties, the latter frequent and often comic. Although the south of Spain had long had an important tourist industry, at that time Galicia was more or less undeveloped in this respect. What hotels there were catered for Spaniards from inland and some Portuguese. A number of well-to-do families from Madrid had villas on the coast, where the women and children spent several months in the summer to get away from the heat of the Spanish tableland, and a few French tourists were beginning to come along the north coast. Inland, however, Santiago de Compostela had been a place of pilgrimage since the twelfth century and therefore had a long tradition of hospitality to foreigners.

We met no one who spoke English or French so we needed our dictionary. We were "en pension" in the hotel and we ate the meals which were put in front of us, often with little idea what we were being offered. Faced for the first time with squid in their own ink topping a white mountain of rice, the children laughed so much that the whole dining room looked to see what had happened. And one course followed another, so how much to eat of each?

The lively fishing village was a small summer resort, and, up the hill behind the town, the peasant farmers and their families lived and farmed as their ancestors had done for centuries. A friendly, cheerful people, they were as curious about us as we about them and they persisted in their questioning in spite of our complete lack of Spanish or the local language, Gallego.

It was on the journey home from that holiday that we first met Roderick Mann, without whose help and encouragement this project would never have got started. He and Ana, his Spanish wife, are an integral part of this story.

Summer after summer we went back to Galicia, and the sun and the welcome of the people warmed us, the beauty of the hills and coastline soothed us and livened our senses too, and the strangeness stimulated us to want to know more about this Galicia – Spain and yet not quite Spanish, a country where the twentieth century with its motor cars and fridges was only just arriving, superimposed on a medieval way of life.

Already on earlier holidays in Ireland and Wales, we had played a game of imagination: shall we come and live here when we retire? What would it be like all the year round? But then it was only a game.

At home in England our normal life went on. We belonged in our community and our children grew up following the normal paths and going through the normal stages. We were involved in many aspects of city life, and behaved, most of the time, in most ways, just about in the way we were expected to behave. Robert's interest in gardening grew and grew, beyond or perhaps more accurately, in a different direction from that of our friends and neighbours. He became more and more interested in unusual and rare plants, in propagation and experiment, in the scientific aspects of horticulture.

His unrest must have grown almost unnoticed, hidden by his genuinely keen interest in his city affairs. Gradually however, circumstances changed and he came to realise that he could retire, and he began to think of the joy there would be in making a new experimental garden in Galicia. Instead of retirement being an end it could be a beginning.

So it was that we went to live in Galicia in February 1970. We sold our house in England and exported our furniture with the intention of making our permanent home there.

This is an account of the venture: how we got started and how we established ourselves in such different surroundings, alternately stimulated and frustrated, soothed, baffled or charmed, and how, in the end, the venture came to an end, the inevitable and painful end to a rich chapter of life.

"Why?" our family and friends asked, and our new neighbours in Spain asked. We explained that Robert wanted to make a garden in a climate which would give him the opportunity to experiment with the growing of a wider variety of plants than was possible in England. To our Spanish neighbours we said, "There is more sun here." Inadequate reasons. Now I think that the real answer was that we were bewitched.

We had thought about the question very seriously for several years. What of our family and friends? Was it right to break up our family home? Now our children were grown up, but would they not still need a base to return to, perhaps even a shelter? Would moving away cut us off from the adult friendship we hoped to establish with them, and from our other friends? Perhaps, but we hoped not. We hoped we could make a new home with other attractions, a place for holidays, where the blend of peace and stimulation might give strength to deal with the everyday working world of their lives. If we were busy and happy, perhaps we should be more worth visiting.

Retirement for most people is one of the major changes of their lives. Our generation was the first to have reason to expect a lot more years to live – bar accidents of course. How best to use those years?

Many people have an urge to start something new but lack the opportunity, or, having the opportunity, lack the means. We found ourselves in the fortunate position of having the urge, opportunity and means. So when we started to look for a piece of land in Galicia, the old game of "shall we live here?" took on new significance.

3

Looking for land

"Antes de facelo, pensao ben." (Gallego saying)
Think before you act.

In August 1966 when we arrived in Vigo we went to lunch with Roderick and Ana Mann and feasted on fresh sardines grilled over an open fire of maize cobs, and sat talking over our idea of buying land for Robert's retirement, when it came.

Roderick had lived and worked for many years in Vigo, and he had explored widely around the countryside. He and Ana were interested and encouraging.

"But why Galicia? Why not Asturias or the south?"

We explained that we liked the people of Galicia, cautious and individualistic. We liked the fertile green countryside which reminded us of the west of Ireland, though sunnier and more colourful, and in contrast to the depopulation in Ireland, bubbling with life. No, we did not want the hot dry climate of the south. Our idea was to look for a property within a radius of about ten miles from Pontevedra, within reach of the coast but not on the coast because of Atlantic wind and rain.

Pontevedra is the administrative capital of the province, a sleepy old town expanding rapidly. The medieval town is a maze of narrow streets and small squares on a hill sloping down to the River Lérez, at the head of a long arm of the sea, one of the *rías* so characteristic of this coast. Granite houses with narrow overhanging balconies, often glass-fronted or with decorative iron railings and gaily flowering plants in pots. The houses of prosperous townspeople or aristocrats carry coats of arms, carved in stone on their austere facades. Down on the river front is the noisy populous market, selling fish from the many small ports on either side of the *ría,* and flowers, fruit, vegetables and meat from the countryside around. Once Pontevedra was the most important fishing and commercial port of Galicia, with a shipbuilding industry too, but the river silted up, and now the town has been left fifty years behind bustling modern Vigo in prosperity, tempo and way of life.

That summer we stayed in Pontevedra, and one day the Manns brought their friend Alfredo to meet us. He knew everything about Pontevedra, they said. He was square, sunburned and very chatty, but sadly we understood very little of what he said. Years later, when I met him again, he sat down and laughed at the memory of how helpless we had been. Yes, he had heard of a property and he would take us to see it, so we set off in a two car convoy; two kilometres up the hill out of the town, down a bumpy lane, past a village washing place, a meadow and on into pine woods. We got out to look and there below us was the blue, blue river curling its way down the valley. Now Alfredo took us to the house through a stone gateway and the owner came out to greet us, a bony brown old man wearing a battered straw hat, and showed us round his *finca.* The word means any property with or without a house.

This property, called *Vista Real* (Royal View) was a sizeable farm, far bigger than we would want. Most of it was woodland, mainly pines, and about twelve acres were cultivated; there were maize fields, tomatoes and kale, and flowers for the market – gladioli, lilies, chrysanthemums and carnations. The house was a great long barn of a building, single storey with storerooms underneath where the ground fell away. Below it was a terrace of vines and an orchard.

As we strolled back to the house, a price was discussed and named – in that order as is normal in Galicia where the price of anything is never clearly stated at the start of negotiations. The price was far too much for us as was the size of the *finca,* so we suggested that perhaps we could buy a small piece of woodland at the far end? But no, the old man was not interested, he wanted to sell the whole place. Wages were too high, he said, and he could not make the cultivation pay; the woodland was unproductive too because the price of wood had dropped. He was tired, his son was not interested, and he wanted to go and live in Pontevedra and spend his afternoons drinking with his friends in a café and watching the world go by.

Back at the hotel we sat on the terrace and discussed what we had seen. Was there any possibility that next year, we could make an offer for a piece of the old man's woodland? If after all he had not managed to sell, if we could find the right piece, if there was water, if and if and if…

"Does it seem real to you?" asked Ana. "Is it a serious search? Or is it a sort of game?"

These were disturbing questions and I woke in the night with a sense of anguish. Was it a betrayal of our home life to be so thrilled by this dream of a Spanish hillside? Could we pack up our settled lives, our lares and penates, our astonishing accumulation of properties?

The following summer, when we came back, Alfredo told us that the *Vista Real* had been sold to a company who were going to set up a model milk farm; they had refused to sell us a small piece. He would continue to make inquiries for us and explained that it was no good going to an estate agency because they did not function like English ones and would certainly cheat us. There was a further difficulty, he said: Galicians never sell anything at the first attempt, nor at the first or second price mentioned, and in any case they think that all foreigners are millionaires. He was sorry he would not have time to help us during the next few days because General Franco was making a visit to Pontevedra and he was on duty to welcome him. So we went out prospecting for ourselves. How naïve we were!

A piece of apparently unused land, overlooking the river upstream from the *Vista Real* caught our eye, and we took compass and tape measure to survey it. We scrambled about an imaginary site for a house and garden, steep rough hillside with a small wood and some meadows below, fronting on the river. A small stream came down the hill and had been diverted to make an elaborate irrigation network. The grass meadows beside the river were lovely and we had a happy afternoon. Angles and sums. A beautiful site – but a pipe dream.

Of course it was a pipe dream. Roderick and Ana came to help us find the owner who had never thought of selling. Anyway the land was owned jointly by a whole family, some of them in Spain but others abroad. They needed that pasture for the cows, and the woman herself had made that drinking place down by the river, and the woodland belonged to someone else who was away abroad. Anyway, since we were people from the great world, we would find ourselves somewhere to build a house and what was it to do with them?

The episode highlighted for us another difficulty about buying land. When someone dies in Galicia, the land is divided between all his sons and daughters, although the one remaining at home and farming it will get a bigger portion. This results in tiny farms with fields and bits of woodland scattered around a district, as each farmer's wife has her inheritance too, maybe miles away. So it is difficult to buy a reasonably sized piece of land because the various owners, who may or may not be of the same family, are unlikely all to agree to sell, or if they do, only at a high, even ridiculous price. Add to this the likelihood that some of the owners may be working in France, Germany, Switzerland or Belgium, or have emigrated to South America. One hears stories of emigrants whose inheritance had been the least productive sand-dune or rocky seashore, since they were not at home to protest. Returning in modern times to visit their families, they discover that their piece of barren land is now immensely valuable whereas their brothers' and cousins' fertile fields inland are worth comparatively little.

We explored hillsides and asked in bars, but made little progress. One *finca* turned out not to be for sale after all; another, in a strange way, was far too expensive because the family had realised that the area was going to develop into a seaside resort soon. Then Roderick asked Casimiro Duran to meet us and the situation changed.

Casimiro is a leading Vigo citizen and comes from an old Pontevedra family. His imagination was fired by our project. "Why not put an advertisement in the newspaper?" he suggested. He would insert it and Roderick would field the replies. If there were any hopeful ones before we left, we could go and look, otherwise he and Roderick would, and if they found a "*finca* we would like ourselves", then they would send for us urgently. He himself fancied seeing us installed in an old *pazo* because

14

it would be likely to have enough land round it. He described the inheritance system in Galicia as "very democratic, but you see, not very practical" because it results in this patchwork of tiny fields with its elaborate mosaic of ownership.

Pazos are a very interesting feature of the Galician countryside. Like manor houses, they are the homes of the gentry, and in earlier times they were the castles of feudal lords. Many are neglected and unoccupied because their owners have gone off to Madrid, keeping their ancestral mansions but only using them for summer holidays. They are big solid houses, with coats of arms carved on their facades and generally a small private chapel, and sometimes with their old castle towers or a modern replica.

On Monday 21st August, we were woken in our hotel bedroom by the phone. Roderick said he had lots of answers to the advertisement, and two of them we should look at immediately. One belonged to a friend of his and was up the hill at Cela, overlooking the Porriño valley; the other was near Pontevedra. He had arranged for us to visit the latter next day. The matter was urgent because we were sailing for England on Thursday.

La Saleta belonged jointly to a numerous family. Three of the sons showed us round that first time, all talking at once which made comprehension extra difficult. A sizeable farm, it had fourteen acres of land, enclosed by a stone wall, and derelict buildings and chapel around a vine-covered courtyard. One of the brothers told me that when Philip II of Spain went adventuring in the Alps, a troop of his soldiers got caught in a snowstorm and nearly died of hunger, and one of them, in gratitude for their safe homecoming, had built the chapel. I never did find any reason to believe this romantic story!

Most of the land had once been cultivated but was now neglected, a tangle of brambles. The *finca* had been terraced and there were plenty of old vines, as in Galicia, grown on trellises supported on granite posts. There was a delightful small wood with old oaks and pines, a large round dovecote, some orange and lemon trees, an *hórreo* (a grain store on stilts), a wine cellar, two wells and an antiquated water pump. Of course it was much too big for us, but the situation was lovely. The hillside sloped down towards a belt of woodland to the south-east, and beyond, half-hidden, was the village backed by hills. There was plenty of water. We could imagine where one would build a new house. One of the brothers suggested that we might sell bits of it to other English people, or even make a golf course!

The following day, Wednesday, Roderick and Ana accompanied us for a second look. It looked even more beautiful than the previous day, but even bigger. What about goats, sheep or a cow? Fantasy or realism? Sums. How much money would it be sensible to sink in such a venture? Would it be too much to manage?

On Thursday the Manns took us to see the property at Cela. There was a little rambling house in a steep garden, surrounded by woodland, perched high up the hill, with a wonderful view over the village in the valley to the mountains beyond. It was called *Lugar del Carballo* (place of the oak tree) and we looked around for some big oak.

"Oh no, not an oak tree," said Roderick's friend Stella. Half English, half Spanish, she talked in a vivid flow of slightly strange English intermingled with Spanish turns of phrase. "My grandfather bought the *finca* and built the house, and he was – how do you call it? – a hard, stiff man, like an oak tree, and all the villagers called him 'oak tree'. His property had no name because it didn't need one; it was known as 'the old oak's place'. We only put up the name later."

I liked the place. One could make a home there at once, unlike La Saleta where there would be five years work before one could be settled. I liked the sense of being at the top of the world. But Robert considered the garden too narrow and steep, and the house was not what we would want but too good to pull down. Besides there was a very serious snag, a mink farm next door. From the access road, the smell was appalling, though that day at least, it did not seem to penetrate to the actual property.

Back at the Manns we discussed the matter all afternoon. We were sailing that evening and must make a decision if either La Saleta or Cela were suitable.

The magnitude of the decision was disturbing. Robert thought Cela would be cramping, and I thought that La Saleta would eat money and take at least five years to develop into anything like a garden, which it did. Robert was angry with me for preaching prudence.

Then suddenly, he decided to go for what he wanted. So, before we left for our boat, we asked Roderick to make an offer for La Saleta on our behalf.

I still have a folder with the other replies to that advertisement but of course we looked at none of them. There were houses by the beach, and a farm up the mountain. There was a piece of land in Vigo itself suitable for building a housing estate. There was a modernised *pazo* with "good windows" and "enough room for 2 families" and another bordering on communal hillside "so more can be taken into cultivation and legally so". I do regret that I never went to find the *finca* "on the banks of the River Lérez founded by Maestre Mateo (the famous sculptor) in the year 1200".

4

February 1968

"Bailar e rascar, todo quer comenzar." (Gallego saying)
Dancing and scratching, everything wants to start.

Throughout that autumn of 1967, Roderick and Casimiro conducted negotiations with the owners of La Saleta. The proceedings were slow, what with bargaining, and also because, at that time, the foreign exchange regulations laid down by the Bank of England had an important bearing on what we could spend on buying land abroad. We had to have the permission of the bank, and obtain foreign exchange by buying property dollars which cost a certain percentage more than the straightforward exchange rate – in effect a form of taxation on buying foreign property.

Finally a price was agreed, the money sent, and the deal concluded, and thus it was that we went to Galicia in February 1968 as the new owners of La Saleta, and had that memorable first meeting with Eugenio and his family.

This was our first visit to Galicia in the spring, and this time we drove from Bilbao along the north coast of Spain, westwards along an apron of green meadows between mountains and sea. After Ribadeo we turned inland up a steep river valley, up and up, until we came out on a bleak, grey tableland of peaty marshes and stunted trees. Then after Lugo the landscape softens and there are rolling hills, and oak, chestnut and birch woods, until approaching the Atlantic coast, the deciduous trees give way to pines and eucalyptus. Ahead of England, spring was bursting out, and we passed catkins and pussy willows, primroses and mimosa in full flower, and, here and there, a tree-sized camellia flowering in a garden.

We were impatient to get to know our new world. The day after our arrival, Roderick and Ana came to help us communicate with Eugenio, who was most anxious that we should understand, and explained everything again, several times, to make sure. So, once more, every inch of the property was inspected.

What about the vines? There were trellises and trellises of them, many of them old and neglected. On Roderick's instructions, Eugenio had already had the best of them pruned and tied up, and now Robert had the debt to settle. Eugenio said that he had worked on them with four other men and therefore we owed him eight hundred pesetas, two hundred each. But what about himself? Robert gave him more, but he gave it back indignantly. No, he did not want any pay for this service. One day, he explained, he might need our help. The same difficulty arose about spraying the vines, as this would need doing in our absence, and also some of the little plants Robert had brought in the trailer would need watering. We wanted to leave some money with Eugenio, at least to pay for the spray, but Eugenio was very proud about money. However, in the end he agreed that he would keep an account of what we owed him for materials and we could pay him when we came. Indeed we needed an interpreter.

By the time we had lived there for some years, we understood better how this neighbour relationship worked. The families living in each small group of houses formed a community who recognised their interdependence. Traditionally, all the families of the group worked together on many of the regular tasks of their farms, planting and gathering in potatoes, grain crops, pruning and picking the grapes. In the past, flax was grown, spun and woven into household linen and clothing, and much of the work was done communally on winter evenings. This had disappeared by the time we came, as had the use of communal bread ovens and small watermills, though old traditions have survived longer in isolated districts. Nevertheless there was, and still is, co-operation with long and laborious jobs such as pruning and tying up vines, and also when a household has illness or special difficulties.

In return the host family cook and serve substantial meals to their helpers.

Thus normally no money is exchanged between neighbours for services rendered. Juan does Pedro a favour and next month or next year, Pedro does one in return, or else brings him a present, a dozen bottles of his best wine perhaps, or a nice piece of the pig they have just killed. The system led to abuse too, as the rich and powerful might come to expect presents in return for the simplest help and might even shirk their obvious duties and responsibilities to their poorer neighbours without what they considered adequate gifts; and as the peasant firmly believed that he would not get fair treatment from the mayor perhaps, or the judge, or even the doctor, without bringing a good present, the abuse was perpetuated.

There is a classic story about a Galician countryman who suggested to his lawyer that it might advance his suit if he sent a good ham to the judge. The lawyer protested: "No, no! This judge is very modern and very honourable, and if you do that, the case will go against you." In due course the case came up and the judge gave judgement in favour of our friend, who said triumphantly to his lawyer as they left the court: "You see what a good ham can do!" "What?" said the lawyer. "You sent one after what I said?" "Yes," said the Galician, "but as I listened to what you said, I sent it in the name of my opponent."

Then what about electricity? The line to the house was only 125 volts and the current was poor because La Saleta was at the end of the line, which came along from the nearest village, hanging from bent and twisted tree-posts and blew off every time there was a storm. How could we get a better supply? Eugenio told us a long and complicated story about how he had quarrelled with the electricity boss. Roderick then delivered him a lecture on the subject of not involving us, as foreigners, in long-established village feuds that were nothing to do with us; we wished to be friends with everyone. However it was perfectly clear that Eugenio did not even want to tell us who to apply to.

Later we did get the question disentangled and it was surprising. The previous priest, who had died some thirty years earlier, was a man of some wealth and influence. He brought electricity to the district and held the concession himself. He had three nieces -there was gossip about them – and one of them married the man in charge of the line and when the priest died, she inherited the business. So we had to apply to them and even they advised us not to try to cook by electricity because it was too unreliable.

That February day we looked everywhere. The buildings consisted of the chapel, gateway, and single storey stone-built rooms and stables around the yard, which was knee-deep in weeds in places and littered with bottles, old shoes and rags. Next to the chapel was a big room with niches in the thickness of the walls, "for bees", Eugenio explained. The bees came and went from the outside through small holes, and, inside, the niches were closed with a wooden board and sealed with cow-dung. Then there was a taller house, built only of wooden beams, lath and plaster. It had been erected in about 1918 to house farm workers, and time and woodworm had made it unusable, even unsafe. In the past the resident caretakers had occupied two tiny rooms and a kitchen at the front of the yard. The main house on the back of the yard, which the family had used, had a large living room with two sleeping alcoves off it, two other small bedrooms, and a kitchen with the traditional stone *lareira,* an open fireplace on a wide stone shelf, built out from the wall, beneath a big canopied chimney. Facing it was a stone seat for winter comfort. Both kitchens had granite sinks with water outlets through the wall, in the one case to the outside, in the other into the adjoining stable.

The rooms were in a terrible condition. The plaster was falling off walls, ceilings, doors and window frames and floors were so worm-eaten that they were disintegrating. The main kitchen wall, built into the slope of the hill, was green with mould and the big stones were running with water.

Most old farmhouses had the stables and possibly the kitchen on the ground floor and the living rooms above, a dryer and warmer arrangement. The toilet, if there was one at all, consisted of a small room with a hole in the floor to the cowshed beneath, thus enabling human and animal excrement to be cleared out together and used to manure the fields – a very practical arrangement. At La Saleta the tall workers' house had one of these, but the family house had a wooden throne on a platform, raised up six steps in the corner of the outhouse, the latter also holding the bread oven. The caretakers' rooms had no provision whatever – in the poorest houses people relieved themselves in a corner of the cowshed. Since then, of course all this has changed and houses have water closets and modern bathrooms. Eugenio installed a bathroom in about 1972.

It had been a long, busy day, and then there was the business of locking up; every door had to be locked with a huge heavy key, all of six inches long; all the windows and shutters shut and fixed in place by iron bars – "Just in case," said Eugenio. We drove back to our hotel in Pontevedra and the Manns missed their train…

That visit we spent twelve days in Galicia, taking a picnic lunch to La Saleta each day. One day we were unlucky because Eugenio's dog found and ate our sandwiches. Eugenio was worried that we had cold lunches and he was sure we would catch chills, so he went home and fetched us a bottle of his own *aguardiente* (burning water), a spirit distilled from the skins and pips of the grapes. It is the local cure for all ills.

I asked Eugenio about their diet. Salt pork, some fish, bread and potatoes, he told me, and of course their own wine. Until recent years these farms were just about self-sufficient, each family keeping a pig, some chickens, a cow, and growing their own onions, turnip tops, carrots and perhaps peas, beans and lettuces. They might grow a few water melons, and have a cherry, plum or apple tree, but they set no great store by the fruit and did not bother to care for the trees. Wine was an integral part of the diet though, and tending the vines a big element in the farming year. In some districts some nice white wine was produced but this was, and still is, for sale or for special occasions, and the normal home drink is the sour red. Eugenio once told me that the three of them living in his house drank three litres a day between them. They did not drink water – "that gives you frogs in your belly."

From time to time Eugenio told me about conditions when he was a child. He remembered when everyone used their *lareira* for cooking. They burned wood and there was often a shortage, so a good deal of pilfering took place. The traditional soup-stew, *caldo gallego*, made of salted pork, potatoes and turnip tops, was cooked in an iron pot suspended by a chain over the fire. He remembered a time when only two families in the hamlet could afford to keep a pig. The others might buy just a little meat from them. During the years we lived in Galicia all this changed. Three small butchers shops have opened in the district and there is fish every morning in the market place. A much greater variety of foodstuffs have become available in the village shops.

The plants Robert had brought to start his dream garden had to be got into the ground and he started a nursery bed. Eugenio worried about their safety: village children would come and steal them or their labels, and his cows would step on them when he brought them to graze, though his cows were not wicked.

I had time to explore, observing, watching, even prying into what was going on. My senses sharpened, colours seemed brighter, smells and sounds clearer. I felt awake as never before. I greeted everyone I passed and of course, I attracted a lot of curiosity and felt very conspicuous. People stopped working in the fields to stare at me or accost me with a torrent of questions. It was especially the older women whose curiosity got the better of their shyness and maybe suspicion. Why had we come? Did we like Galicia? Were we going to grow trees? Flowers? For the market? Were we going to live there all the year round? What, even in winter? The idea that we were going to make a garden and grow plants just for pleasure was, naturally, outside their range of imagination, and I do not think they believed it. What use are plants that you do not eat, or sell? Later we heard that there was a rumour in the area that we must be growing drugs, hidden away among those shrubs. Rich foreigners and very mad!

5

The second week

"Auga corrente non mata a xente." (Gallego saying)
Running water does not kill.

There were several important matters to deal with during the second
week of that visit. We needed to think about the old buildings. Casimiro
Duran recommended a Pontevedra architect, who shall be called
Antonio, and though he spoke neither English nor French, he spoke
slowly and clearly for us, and he listened with much patience to what
we were trying to say.

The floors and interior walls were past saving, he said, but once the
inside of the house was gutted, we could have any arrangement of rooms
we liked. New electrical wiring was essential as now it was dangerous,
and, yes, it was perfectly feasible to put in plumbing and sanitation and
a septic tank. So we sat down under the vines with a drink and Eugenio
joined us, and we discussed what we wanted. Antonio promised to give
us some idea of the cost before we left for England and to send us
details later. He advised using a small local builder and Eugenio said
there were several. Could the conversion be done in time for us to use
the house in August? Quite possibly, even probably. In those days we
believed what we were told about time.

The following day we went to Santiago to pay our buyers' tax to the
lawyer who had dealt with the sale of the property to us, and to complete
the formalities. Eugenio came with us to show us the way, and to help
us negotiate with the previous owners who wanted us to buy some

wine-making equipment they had left in the cellar. Eugenio looked very trim in his suit, white shirt and black beret.

During the drive we added to our store of information. La Saleta had belonged to the aunt of the brothers we knew, called Doña Sofía, who had been considered to be a saint by all in the neighbourhood. Since her death, Eugenio said, the traditional *fiesta*, which used to take place every Whitsunday at La Saleta, had lapsed, and the villagers hoped that perhaps we would revive it.

We had already heard about the *fiesta*, which was what is called a *romería* though it had in fact lost many of the characteristics of a *romería*. These were celebrated all over Galicia, generally at some small chapel or shrine in an outlying place: by the sea, by a spring or on a hill-top. It is thought that the tradition dates from pre-Christian times and that the early Church took over many pagan customs transforming them as best it could. Mass was celebrated in a chapel or in the open air, and people came from miles around, often seeking a cure for illness or the evil eye, bringing picnics, and settling down around the site for a happy day out with dancing, drinking and exchange of news, and certainly opportunities for courting. Except in a few cases, much of the flavour has been lost from these *romerías* with the arrival of motor cars, dance floors and doctors.

The name is derived from *romero*, in medieval times a pilgrim to Rome. The pilgrims who went to the Holy Land were known as *palmeros* (palmers) because they used to carry palm leaves on their return, as proof of their accomplished journey. The *peregrinos* (pilgrims) were those who made the pilgrimage to Santiago de Compostela; they returned wearing scallop shells in their hats.

La Saleta is the Spanish for La Salette, a small place near Grenoble in France, where in 1846 the Virgin Mary is said to have appeared to two children on a mountainside. The resulting cult spread widely through the Catholic world, mainly as a missionary order. Our chapel's wooden altarpiece had a statue of the Virgin with the children gazing up at her from either side. It was not beautiful but had a certain rustic charm.

We do not know how old the La Saleta *romería* is. We do know that the chapel was built, or perhaps rebuilt, in 1867-8 by Doña Sofía's father, and that it was then that it was dedicated to the Virgin of La Saleta, but it seems possible that the *romería* dates from long before that. Doña Sofía's father had a *pazo* in Cambados, where he lived, so one wonders why he built a chapel attached to his farm in the country. But in spite of a good deal of research, I never found any evidence of an older chapel, or older *romería*, nor any corroboration of the legend about Philip II's soldiers.

The earliest house on the site was built by Sofía's great-great grandfather, Mateo, around 1721, and he had inherited the property, then about half its present size, from his mother's family who descended from a noble family of the area.

Eugenio did not know Santiago very well since he only went there to horse fairs once or twice a year, so it was difficult to find the notary's office. Then we had to wait in a passageway while all sorts and conditions of people wandered to and fro. And when we were ushered into the notary's office, it transpired that the documents still had to be fetched from the Land Registry, so we waited again. The scene might have come out of a Dickens novel: the shabby crowded office where every surface was piled high with books, papers, files, all very dusty. The bald, fat little notary bustled about, affable in a vague way, but preoccupied, excited.

Now a curious change of roles took place. The previous day we had understood the architect much better than we understood Eugenio, but this day Eugenio acted as interpreter because the notary muttered and we did not understand a word he said. Eugenio repeated everything very slowly.

That business concluded, Eugenio took us to the vendors' house and acted as go-between in the tricky negotiation about the price of the old wine press and barrels. We sat round a table and the young daughter of the house served biscuits and *aguardiente*. There was a long desultory conversation about crops. Then, would they name a price? No, what would Don Roberto offer? 8,000 pesetas? No, no, that would not do at all; they would not accept less than 10,000 for such good equipment, and only as little as that because we were the new owners of the *finca*. In the ordinary way, bargaining would have gone on for a long while, interspersed with talk of other matters, but Eugenio made a speech, explaining that Don Roberto, being English, did not understand Gallego bargaining, and therefore wanted a straight price.

At this stage it was obvious that we could not ask Eugenio's advice; he was both embarrassed and enjoying his role. So we settled for 10,000 pesetas and I think Eugenio approved. We should have heard all about it on the way home if he had not.

Then there was the problem of the water channel, the *mina*, which was evidently blocked. Water was of prime importance in the countryside because there was no piped water, nor any supply arrangements, and we had taken the question carefully into account when we were looking for land. La Saleta had two big wells, but the spring water had always been used for drinking and we were, rightly as it turned out, doubtful about the purity of the well water. The spring was in the woodland, some fifty metres up behind the house, and the rights to the water had been written into our deeds. The previous August it had been flowing in a steady trickle and we had been assured that it never dried up, but now there was no flow at all and obviously it was the time of year when there should be the greatest flow.

Up in the wood, the spring was accessible at the bottom of a deep, stone lined well-like structure, whose opening was covered over, for safety, by two huge granite slabs. There were iron handles fixed to the stones of the lining to form a sort of ladder down. At the bottom, though I myself never ventured down to look, the spring bubbled up and then flowed through a simple earthen tunnel all the way down under the woodland, under the track, and under our wall, where it emerged and continued on its way in an open cement channel into a small cistern. From there it ran through two pipes in an upright granite headstone to spout out over an open stone washing tank.

"I can bring a man who knows these channels," said Eugenio. "He can crawl up the tunnel to see what has happened. It must be blocked somewhere. On Sunday – you will be sure to be here, won't you?"

So, on Sunday, Moncho came, a cheerful, square, young man, wearing jeans and a straw hat. He lived nearby, he told us, and he had been brought up by his grandmother who had been caretaker at La Saleta. Oh yes, he had often been up the channel! He worked in a quarry, he said; once he had worked in a bakery, but that was no good – all night work, so he could not go out.

"Only suitable for married people," he said.

He showed us that he had a torch, and a knife in case of snakes. Eugenio suggested that he should take Robert's pick to clear fallen earth, and we all went up to the foot of the wall where the tunnel disappeared into darkness. Moncho wriggled his way in. The rest of us walked round and up to the well-mouth, and waited. And waited.

Eugenio observed thoughtfully that he himself was too fat to get through that tunnel, and Moncho was thinner. I thought, to myself, that he was as afraid of it as I was – but, after all, Moncho had been there before. Our hearts in our mouths, we waited.

"Ah!" said Eugenio suddenly. "He's whistling."

I could hear nothing. We waited. Then, yes, we could really hear whistling and it came nearer and nearer, until there was Moncho at the bottom, shining his torch into the pool of water to show us it really existed. A shouted discussion ensued between him and Eugenio, and then he came climbing up the staircase of iron handles. At the top, Eugenio helped him out with a final heave, and he emerged, filthy-dirty, but grinning and still wearing his straw hat.

Yes, a good deal of earth had fallen and he had only just managed to squeeze his way through. Yes, he could find men to help, and they would be able to clear the channel: perhaps six men working with a rope and bucket, three below and three above.

What about insurance? Suppose the whole roof fell in and someone broke a leg – or was killed – said Eugenio. We must take out a special temporary insurance for the men. He was most insistent, and we were certainly not disagreeing, for the whole plan seemed to us highly dangerous. Even if insurance was expensive, the two men thought it would be less expensive than employing a builder whose men would already be insured, and much less expensive than compensation if an accident did occur.

Who would come? And when? They were not ready to commit themselves to an estimate of how many days' work it would need, but Eugenio was quick to say, and demonstrate by mime, that he would supervise the work to make sure the workers did not spend their time sitting down. So it was agreed. Eugenio would give us a list of the men who would help, and we would go to the insurance office and take out a special short-term policy to cover them.

As we walked away from the wood, we realised that Moncho had left the pick at the bottom of the hole.

Next day we went to the insurance office in Pontevedra and got some forms. We had no idea how to fill them in, nor had the hotel manager when we consulted him. Eugenio suggested we should ask Antolín, as he worked in the *Ayuntamiento* and he would be sure to know.

Two days before we left, we thought we had nearly settled the matter. The forms were completed except for the workers' signatures and identity card numbers. I looked for Eugenio and found him tying up his vines, and he climbed down off his rickety old stepladder to examine them. One of the men lived some way away, he said, but he would see him on market day; however Moncho had no identity card.

"Why not?" I asked.

"Because he doesn't work."

"But he told me he worked in a quarry."

"That isn't work – that's private."

"What do you mean?"

"He works for his uncle so they don't pay taxes or anything," explained Eugenio, and he went on to say that you only needed an identity card to go travelling or to work in a factory or in public employment, and that anyway it cost 100 pesetas, so no one would get one if he did not need to. Then he told us all over again how important it was to have this insurance. Suppose the roof fell in and someone…

I gave up and left the papers with him. Please would he finish them off for us and take them to the insurance office.

The days had rushed by. Robert had finished his planting, we had opened a bank account, and we had discovered how to pay our land taxes; we had taken some well water to the Sanitary Department for analysis, and had found the local electricity boss and arranged for him to extend the 220 volt line to the house.

Our last evening the architect came to the hotel to see us. He had worked out an approximate estimate of the cost of doing up the best part of the old house, mending the walls and roof as necessary, and remaking the inside with new floors and interior walls to provide a sitting room, bedroom, bathroom and kitchen. We promised to study it and let him know as soon as possible, as we wanted to have the work done in time for our summer holiday.

Next morning at La Saleta we had the last clearing up to do and to say goodbye. We walked all round with Eugenio, and Robert showed him exactly where he had put in plants. Some of them would need watering and would his daughter perhaps do that? Celina and María-Ester were fetched to look, and there were elaborate assurances that we could depend on them to look after everything.

I asked Celina about the pile of priests' vestments which I had found in a worm-eaten cupboard. Some were beautiful, and there were pieces of chapel silver too. Celina suggested that she should take all these things to their house to look after, and that she should wash everything washable, even the Virgin's wig, which she wears on the day of the *romería*. It certainly needed washing, but sadly it did it no good!

We had intended to give back the nearly full bottle of *aguardiente* when we handed over the keys, but another one was pressed into our hands for the journey. The two bottles caused bother with the English Customs as we had no idea what proof the spirit might be.

When we arrived home we sent a picture postcard and some weeks later we had a reply:

"*Señor* Don Roberto and Doña Margarita…all is well. Now about the *mina*. The papers Antolín got ready for you and you signed are all wrong, they tell me in Pontevedra, so nothing can be done until you come. Or do you want me to look for *mina* experts to ask for a price for doing it?…"

During the summer we heard from the architect that Eugenio and a friend – Moncho, we supposed – had cleared out the *mina* channel by themselves, and got the water running. There had been no accident.

6

Summer holiday

"En agosto fago bon reposo." (Gallego saying)
In August I have a good rest.

Now our dream was taking on a certain reality, and planning went forward in earnest. It was soon obvious that no building work was likely to start at once, as Antonio had to draw up plans and send them to us in England, and we had to answer with our comments – a long and difficult letter in Spanish, with the aid of dictionary and grammar book. After that builders had to be found and estimates submitted.

However, now very keen and hopeful, we collected together some furniture, domestic implements and a small new refrigerator, and shipped them to Vigo for the renovated old house. We had a leaflet in Spanish, obtained from the Spanish Embassy in London which set out the import regulations, and we understood that furniture to furnish a holiday house in Spain could be imported from abroad duty free, provided the house was not let nor the furniture sold within the following two years. These things would be useful during our summer holiday – if they arrived in time – and they could then be stored in one of the outhouses while building work was in progress. So we imagined, but we were very innocent in those days and had no idea of the pitfalls.

We arrived, five of us, early in August with the car and trailer piled high with sleeping bags, billy cans and camp beds. We set up our beds on the best areas of floor and camped in the old rooms which Celina had swept for us. We bought a butane gas cooker and obtained a gas cylinder, and then we could cook. We washed up in a bowl in the rough granite sink and threw the vegetable peelings out of the window to join the piles of rubbish, bottles, old clothes and sardine tins, which lay rotting under the lush vegetation.

The water from the *mina* was running nicely now, but all the water for the house had to be carried a hundred yards or so from the outlet pipe above the stone washing tank. After the first few days we realised that it would be easier to wash ourselves, our clothes, the vegetables, and to gut the fish in or beside the water tank than to carry water indoors. So the boys siphoned the water out of the tank and cleaned out the mud, leaves and frogs from the bottom, and once it had refilled, we had a shallow bathing pool but, as in the garden of Eden, there were snakes, which would slither suddenly out of the pipe and splash down into the water.

One morning early, I was stripped naked washing out there when I had a curious feeling that I was watched and turned to look. An old man and his dog were making off, as fast as their legs could carry them, down our land. Had he ever seen a whole naked woman before? I later found out that he was an old bachelor quarryman, who had got in the habit of taking a short cut across our land on his way to work, and many years later I was told that the story, with presumably a strong warning, had spread rapidly through the village.

We discussed the idea of digging a latrine trench, but the ground was too hard and the family too lazy, so we continued as we had begun "each to his own spade", and there was no shortage of hillside and bushes. At first it was hard work even to dig a little hole in the dry ground, but our technique improved and, apart from occasional fuss about lost trowels, the system worked satisfactorily.

Clearing up the rubbish lying about the *finca* was a major chore. At that time there were no arrangements whatever for rubbish collection in the countryside. In earlier times, before plastic and tins, there would have been no rubbish, and bottles were re-used. We burned everything that could be burned, and took the rest in carton loads to the open rubbish dump in the outskirts of the town, – a horrible smelly place, often burning and constantly besieged by seagulls and gypsies.

That holiday we bought food just when we passed suitable shops.

A fish woman came to the door most days, carrying a big basket on her head, which was often so heavy that she could not lift it up again without help. She was about five foot tall and stout, with a swaying waddling walk that must have developed over the years as a result of her haste and the weight of the basket. She would come round the corner of the house and let out a piercing shriek: "Doña Margarita! Doña Margarita!" If I were slow to appear, she would greet me indignantly: "Didn't you hear me call?!"

Here I should introduce Lolita. She and her mother ran the village shop, which was known for miles around and sold a great variety of things, all on a very small scale. It muddled her when I wanted as much as half a kilo of coffee; she ground the beans in an enormous mincing machine and her customers bought 100 grams at a time. When we arrived, the shop was open 365 days of the year, from eight in the morning, when the milk came in from the farms, was measured and the quantity recorded, then collected by the milk factory lorry, until nine o'clock at night when the last customer had run in to buy something for supper. The door stood open in all weathers and the floor was of stone, so it was not surprising that both Lolita and her mother suffered from sore feet, chilblains and rheumatism.

From the very beginning Lolita welcomed us and helped us; I think it was due to the sponsorship – for that was what it was – of Eugenio and Lolita that we were accepted so well in the village. Not all foreigners in country villages have such easy relationships with their neighbours. The shop was the heart of the village, the news centre too, and Lolita knew more even than the priest about what went on. She acted as welfare worker too, dispensing a certain amount of discreet charity and helping people in need. I often consulted her and her advice and opinion was always sincere and valuable. In later years she would ask my opinion about the modern world that was so rapidly affecting country life.

In the summer of 1975, Lolita decided that they might shut the shop on Sunday afternoons, as the doctor had been pressing her to do. She dithered and dithered because she felt it her duty to serve her public, and she worried that they would still come wanting to buy things. Finally I gave the matter a push by writing a notice for her to pin up: "From next Sunday, this shop will shut…" She was ridiculously grateful to me as she had found herself unable to take such a drastic step, but, "We'll only put it up next week, Doña Margarita."

In the summer of 1998, her mother incurably ill, and, her own state pension due, Lolita decided to retire, and the shop shut for ever.

The post was in the hands of the carpenter, Ventura, Lolita's brother-in-law. Lolita's husband, Jorge, was the schoolmaster, his brother Antolín worked in the *Ayuntamiento*, Ventura and José were postmen-carpenters. Thus the family were dominant in the village, respected and sometimes resented. The Post Office consisted of a locked cupboard in a corner of the carpenters' workshop. In those days the post arrived on the bus from Pontevedra at one o'clock, the bus stopped outside the shop, Ventura ran to meet the conductor who handed over the locked leather bag, and the bus went on its way. Ventura ran back to his workshop, sorted and dealt out letters to the small queue of hopeful, waiting people. He had the obligation to deliver telegrams and "urgents", and anything uncollected at the end of the week he took to Mass on Sunday to deliver. Of course, if you looked for your post at some different time, Ventura and José might be out planting potatoes, or mending someone's roof. Alas! Some years later a new, "improved" system of mail delivery to the villages was introduced by the powers-that-be in Madrid and it worked much less well. Now, of course, as I write, the whole system has been truly modernised and letters are delivered to houses.

We felt very close to the countryside that summer. Eating outside under the vines, washing at the water tank, all such activities gave time to contemplate the scenery, notice wild flowers and birds, observe the changing light. We were always particularly aware of the sky at La Saleta, a much wider expanse than we had ever had in an English town. Here there were constant changes of the shapes and colours of clouds and variations in the clarity and texture of the light. At night two different kinds of cricket buzzed and sang. There were butterflies and little lizards, and some beautiful big green lizards came out to sun themselves on top of walls. There were bats in the stables and a little owl could often be seen, even in daylight, sitting on a granite post, cursing and swearing at passing cats.

Not all was delightful. One day when we were out, some animal got into the kitchen and neatly sucked out the inside from five eggs, leaving a pile of empty shells. Then there were the mice, everywhere, attacking any food left accessible. We hung up the bread in a bag hooked to a nail in a beam, but the mice climbed down and ate a hole in the bag. We put cheese in a tightly closed plastic box, but the mice ate a hole, three inches in diameter, through the plastic.

All this while we had had no news of our furniture, so we went to the shipping agents to enquire. The answer was, "No!" The customs officers had said we were tourists and therefore did not need furniture. Stalemate.

Back at La Saleta we studied the leaflet more carefully and thought we understood where we had gone wrong. We ought to have a letter from our local mayor to say we owned land, and we ought to have written to the Head Customs Officer in Madrid asking permission to import furniture for our holiday house. We could do nothing but try again. Meanwhile the customs shed would, no doubt, be drier than our outhouses.

Antonio came bringing the estimates from the three builders Eugenio had suggested; now which to choose? Eugenio was fetched for consultation, and Antonio tried to get his real opinion. Galicians are renowned for not answering questions directly.

"One of these estimates is quite inadequate," said Antonio. "There are no proper details and I don't understand it. Why hasn't he made a proper estimate?"

"Well," said Eugenio, "it's like this. The chap has never done any work for an architect before and he is afraid. He thinks nothing will ever be right and so the house will never be finished."

Eugenio had been dubious about employing an architect – "What for? They cost a lot of money and don't do anything, not any real work!" – but had now acquired a great respect for Don Antonio.

"What about the other two then? One estimate is very much higher than the other. Why?"

Eugenio answered that both were very good chaps, very good workers, very honest and good friends of his. He could recommend either with all his heart, but of course all sorts of things could go wrong, and we mustn't take his word for it, but the one he thought most of was the one who was almost a neighbour, from just across the valley. Antonio pointed out that this man's estimate was much the higher one.

"Well," said Eugenio, "he did say he might consider coming down. Perhaps I could talk to him…"

"Make no mistake," said Antonio, very firmly and slowly, so we should all understand. "We shall accept the lowest estimate, and we are going to make up our minds in the next day or two."

Eugenio agreed to tell his friend to lower his estimate and quickly too, if he wanted the job.

There followed a long talk about the new house, where to site it, water, electricity, septic tank, et cetera. We remembered the snakes and asked about them.

"No," said Antonio. "The snakes of Galicia are not lethally poisonous, not these water snakes anyway – but you would be quite ill if one bit you."

Before the end of our stay we had a good deal to discuss with Eugenio, which took a long time, not only because of language difficulties, but because of the digressions. Yes, he would look after our grape harvest and the wine. The barrel needed mending or we might need a new one. He brushed aside talk of bottles and corks – you keep the wine in the barrel and draw it off as you want it.

The honey, yes, he would send for an expert who used to come round every year, to take the honey. We must buy a large five-litre earthenware pot, of the correct shape – no, glass would not do.

In subsequent years we saw the taking of the honey. It was dramatic. The niches in the thickness of the outer wall of the beehive room were about twenty inches square, with small holes leading through the wall to the outer world through which the bees came and went. Inside, the openings were closed by wooden boards and sealed each year, after the honey had been taken, with a good smear of cow dung. To take the honey, the men lit a fire of rosemary branches inside the room to make smoke and so drive the bees outside. Then they set to work cutting out, as fast as possible, chunks of hive, which they took down to the wine cellar. There, behind tightly closed doors, they squeezed the honey out of the comb by hand, a very wasteful process.

When we told Eugenio that we were trying to get some furniture for the house, which had come by ship from England but had got stuck in the Vigo Customs, he was horrified.

"Can't you say the furniture is for me?" he asked.

"Oh no! That would be worse. Even if they did let it come into the country at all, there would be an enormous amount of duty to pay."

Eugenio thought for a moment. Then he said, "Well, I used to know a man who fixed things – difficult matters, you understand. You had to pay him a lot of money, of course. He once fixed a very important matter for me – he was good for getting hold of false papers too, I believe. Shall I try and find out if he is still practising?"

"No, thank you very much. Not for the moment. We'll see what we can do in London. Anyway you see, because we are foreigners, we have to be specially careful what we do."

Eugenio said that, yes, he understood that. But didn't the Customs charge a terrible lot for keeping things in their warehouse? So he had heard. He had heard a story about a man who was coming on a ship from the Argentine to revisit his family in Galicia, but he died on the way, and his body got put in the Vigo Customs' *depósito*, just like our furniture. When his family got to hear about it, it cost a dreadful lot of money to recover the body.

"In any case," he went on, "it doesn't do to die away from home. If you die in a hospital, maybe your relatives don't hear for several days, because visiting days are only twice a week, so then there are the hospital *depósito* charges to pay, and then you have to pay money to the parish priest of every parish you pass through on the way home, so it comes very expensive. So when the doctors know someone is dying in a hospital they tell the relatives, who quickly arrange to take him home to die."

It was time to leave again. Eugenio and Celina were full of curiosity to know just how we had been living in the dilapidated old house, and they came to inspect every detail inside the house and in the beehive room where we were stowing the things we were leaving. Eugenio insisted that everything, clothes, books, linen and boots, had to be put in sacks and hung from nails in the beams, so that mice neither ate them nor nested in them. The mice in Galicia are special.

7

Winter 1968/9

"Los escarmentados veñen os avisados." (Gallego saying)
Punishment brings wisdom.

Eugenio wrote us long letters that winter. They always started like this: "Dear Don Roberto and family, I hope that when you get this your health will be good. Ours good for the moment."

He wrote for money because the electricity man had come with a bill and was threatening to cut us off. So we sent money at once, explaining that the man had said he would bring the bill before we left. Then he wrote to report that they were picking the grapes, and to ask whether we wanted our *aguardiente* white or yellow, the latter with herbs. He said that the builders and architect were still arguing.

Then he wrote again for money to pay the men who were working with him clearing away the weeds, brambles, and granite posts of old vine trellises. "I had not thought there were so many. In the house they have made the concrete floor and ceiling, and now they are working on top of the roof putting on tiles. They are hurrying."

And then, on the 15th January: "Don Roberto, I am writing to tell you that we have finished the work outside La Saleta and it looks very beautiful. The neighbours who pass by think so too. The house is getting on well…"

On 26th January we wrote to him to say that we expected to arrive on 20th February in the evening, and asked him to leave some firewood near the door so we could make a fire.

During the winter we started fresh moves to obtain our furniture. We got some notes for the "guidance of British subjects intending to settle in Spain" issued by the British Embassy in Madrid. (Here I should explain that though many foreigners had settled in the south of Spain, very few had done so in Galicia.) Now we could understand clearly that we had set about the matter in quite the wrong way. So on 26th November, Robert wrote to the General Directorate of Customs in Madrid, enclosing a copy of the deeds of the *finca* and a list in duplicate of our things. He did not, of course, say that they were already stuck in the Vigo Customs.

From the *Dirección General de Aduanas,* Madrid, 2nd December, 1968.

"Today we have written the following to the Vigo Customs: 'According to the request of Mr R.G., of British nationality, that we should authorise the duty-free importation of furniture and used effects belonging to him, for use in a house which he has bought...for holiday use, this Head Office...has agreed to authorise you to carry out the requested clearance, under the following conditions:

1   Only for the furniture and effects on the attached list, and only for those which have really been used.

2   With presentation of the appropriate financial guarantee for the amount of customs duty. For the cancellation of the before-mentioned guarantee, the interested party will have to present to the Customs, at the right time, a certificate sent by the *Ayuntamiento* in whose district the house is situated, in which it is certified that the furniture and effects concerned have remained in the house for two years. Sent to you for your information."

Roderick wrote on 15th December: "I saw the agent yesterday and discussed the possibility of getting the furniture released by the end of the year – this year – but he sees many snags and thinks it more likely to be the middle of January, at the earliest. Financial guarantee – yes, it is for your bank to make the guarantee. I asked the agent if he had any idea of the amount and he said none – it depended on the Customs. And this is where the snags begin. New unused equipment may be refused or very heavily charged. They may require all the cases to be opened for examination and calculation of customs charges on each item."

He wrote again on 7th February: "Just back from Vigo…well, the agent says that the Customs require your valuation of each item in the cases…I do not consider that the clearance can be done before you arrive. He says that after receipt of your declared values it will be at least a week before they release it."

Our limited grasp of Spanish was severely taxed by all this; only Roderick wrote in English and whatever were all these household items called? It is easy to be wise after the event. Obviously we were very naïve in this matter, not understanding the problems of dealing with the bureaucracy of another country. We had also been precipitate in sending off our things. On the other hand it was very strange that it had proved so difficult to understand, step by step, where we had gone wrong and what we should do next. After all, Roderick had lived for twenty years in Vigo and spoke fluent Spanish, so one might have supposed that the agent could have said at once: "These foreigners have set about this without understanding the regulations, so now they will have to do this and this." It was only after we had eventually got our properties that we discovered that it was forbidden to import new electrical appliances such as a refrigerator into Spain. In the end they had only released our things as a favour to Roderick who had once done a favour to the Vigo Chief Customs Officer!

8

Rain and frustrations

"Auga de febreiro, fai o palleiro." (Gallego saying)
February rain makes the haystack.

Our visit to Galicia in February 1969 began badly. We travelled by car-ferry to Lisbon and the crossing was so rough that the boat arrived twelve hours late in Lisbon. Next day, we drove northwards through Portugal in torrents of rain, and, being very tired, stopped for a night just across the Spanish frontier instead of pushing on to La Saleta in the dark. It was a good thing we did.

We were to have three weeks at La Saleta and were looking forward to spending them in the newly modernised little house, which would mark a big step forward. However, there was an additional reason, that year, for not wanting to stay in a hotel: 1969 was one of the years when the British government limited the amount of money which could be used for holidays abroad: so much per person per year, and so much per car per visit, and we intended to stretch our allowance for the year to cover both a spring and a summer visit. Hence the need for strict peseta economy.

So we arrived at La Saleta about midday. Eugenio appeared to greet us almost before we had stopped the car; he had expected us the day before and was worried. The telegram we had sent arrived two days later.

"The house isn't finished," he told us. "The builder had flu so work stopped for a week and then it has rained and rained so they could not work, but how beautiful it is going to be!"

41

Not only was it not finished – it was far from finished and we were dreadfully disappointed.

The sad truth is that nothing, or almost nothing, is ever finished on time in Galicia, and no one would really expect it to be. Intentions are good, hopes are high, but something always happens to cause endless delays It is not only at village level that this happens: when we built a new house and employed the biggest firm of builders in the area, they lost interest during the finishing stages because they had taken on some more prestigious work.

We visited Antonio in his new office. It was not finished either. "Like your house," he said ruefully but fatalistically.

In Galicia many people work very hard indeed and often extremely long hours, but what they achieve seems sometimes disproportionately little considering the effort they have put in. We found that we had to relax and accept this state of affairs or we would go mad with frustration, and yet the very fact that everyone accepts it as normal and inevitable perpetuates it.

Eugenio hastened to show us the house: new pale red roof tiles, cleaned and re-pointed stone walls. Inside the layout was excellent. The original kitchen and passage had become a beautiful sitting room, with the *lareira*, now cleaned up, as its focal point. A new French window opened out on to a jungle of brambles, it is true, but there under the huge old arbutus beside the *hórreo*, one day we would have a small patio garden. A few windows were in place but no doors, electric wires stuck out here and there, and there was no plumbing whatsoever, nor signs of plumbing.

It was obvious we could not occupy the house so what next? We unloaded the car and Eugenio and Celina rushed to help us stack our luggage in the two small caretakers' rooms on the front where building work had not yet started. Rain poured down and everything got muddled.

Eugenio had picked our grapes and made wine, so we had a glass all round to celebrate our safe arrival; it was very sour indeed. Celina had swept up the caretakers' old kitchen and made a big wood fire on that *lareira* there for us, and she suggested that we fetch the gas cooker from the beehive room and make ourselves an improvised kitchen. Then she ran off home and came back bearing a large sponge cake she had baked for us.

We sorted ourselves out, found plates and cups and utensils from the packed-up cartons. Mice had got into all the boxes and left their droppings, even inside the oven, so we were thankful that Eugenio had insisted on hanging up clothes and bedding. Lunch at last! Fried eggs, bread and fruit, and Celina's cake.

The fire in the old kitchen was cheering, but much of its warmth was lost because there was no window, and the small skylight in the roof let in only a gleam of light, so we had to have the top half of the door open. By six o'clock we had set up a working arrangement in the kitchen, and Robert had inspected his plants and admired the clearing work which had been done in our absence. So we asked Eugenio where we could rent a room nearby.

"Well yes," he said. "But no, you wouldn't like it! Anyway there is no bathroom." So we drove down to Cambados and asked for a room in the Casa Rosita, the small hotel where we had had meals in the past. Yes, they could take us for 130 pesetas a day for room, breakfast and dinner – about sixteen shillings in those days – and we were relieved to think that not too many of our precious pesetas would be spent. The hotel was clean, simple and chilly, and we were the only guests.

We had experienced Galician rain during our previous visits and something of the penetrating damp that accompanies it, but it was only in that early spring of 1969 that we really lived with it. The climate of Galicia is temperate and rainy like that of Cornwall or the West of Ireland, though the hours of sunshine are about three times those of London. Near the coast there are seldom frosts or very high temperatures, but the average rainfall is sixty inches a year and most of this falls in the winter months, blown in from the south-west by Atlantic gales. It may rain for days or weeks, or for half an hour. Once we had fourteen inches of rain in fifteen days, sweeping across the valley in diagonal drifts, the water streaming off the hills, washing away the topsoil and scoring deep channels in its path. Then La Saleta's house felt like Noah's ark.

In the old days, the Galicians had rain capes made of reeds but the modern style of protection is the umbrella. Countrymen go about carrying theirs unfurled and hooked into their coat collars at the back, even when riding a bicycle, horse or tractor. When it rains they manage to ride along holding them open over their heads. Cow minders sit or stand for hours under them. In shops and offices there is always a large pot beside the entrance for the parking of these essentials, and the repair shop does a brisk trade.

Next day, Saturday 22nd February, we went back up to La Saleta, and, while Robert attended to his plants, I made the first of many expeditions to our village telephone exchange, to phone Roderick. No, no more news of our furniture, he said, but he would try stirring up the agent again in the hope that we might get delivery before we left this time.

In those days it was a manual exchange, and the two sisters who ran it sat in turns at the switchboard, behind a sliding glass window, from nine in the morning till eleven at night, and one of them slept beside it at night to put through emergency calls for the doctor or priest. We found phoning in Spanish very difficult for several years, and, if necessary, Carmen or Margot would do the talking for us, and send or receive messages. The lines were often bad or unobtainable.

During that Saturday night, Robert developed a fever with noisy breathing and a painful cough and we were alarmed. The hotel owner called a doctor for us and he gave a prescription. When I took this to the chemist it turned out to be for injection, as was normal in Spain, as we discovered later. However, the chemist reluctantly agreed to give me a similar medicine to be taken by mouth.

Now we were disappointed, discouraged and depressed; the year before we had been too euphoric, too pleased with our adventure, and too cock-sure that we could arrange matters to our satisfaction. We had to learn not to set ourselves, or other people, time targets, nor to be upset when these could not be met. Does one ever really learn? "Tomorrow is another day" is a useful saying but *mañana* can mean "not today", "sometime" or even only "perhaps".

However, by Wednesday Robert was better, the weather too, and so were our spirits. We settled into a routine of spending the days at La Saleta. I cooked simple hot meals, wrote letters, made bonfires of rubbish and attacked bramble thickets while Robert worked with his plants.

We kept our fire going, on the old kitchen *lareira,* so we had a warm corner to shelter from rain and endless builders' problems.

Our builder, José, was a cheerful and enthusiastic young man employing twelve men. Now they would finish quickly, quickly, he assured us. We arranged to spend our second week at the Casa Rosita.

Now indeed we saw progress. Manuel, the plumber, appeared and with his mate set to work to bring the *mina* water across to the house. They dug a hole where they supposed the channel flowed under the track way, and this effort was crowned with success as they found an old stone inspection chamber and cleared so much earth out that both spouts poured forth water and the cistern overflowed. All the workmen stopped work to admire this abundance, exclaiming with surprise and delight.

I find in my diary that Tuesday was a day of great progress and activity: "Bath, et cetera, have been delivered and a lot of piping and drain pipes, electricians are hard at work with yards of trailing wire and shouting of '*Vale, vale*' (OK, OK). A hole has been dug in the earth floor of the wine cellar for the cold-water tank and another hole, down the hillside, for the septic tank. José is rushing around like a pleased puppy, reporting progress each time he meets either of us."

On Wednesday the plumbing team were hard at work. We went to look at what they were doing and found Manuel and his mate in their hole by the *mina* channel. Manuel had a rope tied round his waist and this was fastened to the end of a long alkathene pipe, so, crawling up the tunnel to the spring, he could put it in place. We asked whether this did not frighten him and his mate answered cheerfully as Manuel disappeared from sight: "I wouldn't go. He's afraid but he won't say so! He'll do anything for money." A disturbed bat flew out of the hole.

By Friday of this second week some tiling of the kitchen had been done, the new cold-water cistern was neatly lined with cement, and some doors had arrived. José announced proudly that we would be able to move in the following week.

We had brought door handles from England and when the front door was hung, it was found that there was not quite enough room for the handle against the granite surround, so Luis, the stonemason was sent for and worked for a whole morning cutting back the door jamb by about two inches from top to bottom.

During our earlier visits to Spain we wondered why we could always hear the tapping of stone cutters. Surely, we thought, they could not all be making tombstones? Now we began to understand what a long time it takes to cut stone at all, let alone shape the stones to build a house, and, later, when we built a new stone house, we got to know the stonemasons well. They showed us the whole sequence of cutting, shaping, polishing and then fitting each stone into its appointed place, and this gave us an altogether different conception of the work involved in building such monuments as medieval cathedrals. Since we went to live in Galicia, stonemasons have become increasingly scarce, and it would no longer be possible to build in hand-cut stone. The work is slow and hard, and needs years of practice to learn, and now the young men are not willing to serve so long an apprenticeship.

So as Luis worked on the door jamb, the electricians made holes in the walls and the plumbers made holes in the cement floors, and the air resounded to tapping and banging in several different keys and tempos, accompanied by shouting and singing. Spaniards like a lot of noise.

The weather had improved; it was warmer, sunny, but like an English April with cold winds, drifting clouds, sudden showers. There was pandemonium in the house, but I couldn't go right away in case I was needed for some decision. Robert was completely absorbed in his gardening. So I sat in the sun and watched the clouds throw their moving shadows on the hills across the valley. And anxieties assailed me.

9

More rain

"*Cando chove moito, moito, siñal que va escampar logo, logo.*"
(Gallego saying)
When it rains a lot, a lot, it's a sign that it will clear up later,
later.

By now we had been in Galicia for nearly two weeks and our furniture
was still stuck in the Vigo Customs. Already at the beginning of the
second week, we had visited the agent to enquire, but he received us
brusquely. The customs officer was ill, he said, and nothing could be
done until he recovered. So it was a nice surprise when, on Friday 7th
March, Roderick phoned us at the Casa Rosita to tell us the good news
that our things were to be released the following Monday. Would we
go to Vigo the following day, Tuesday, to arrange for their transport?
The telephone was distant and crackling so Robert could hear no more
details.

So we made plans. Encouraged by the progress of the house, and by
warmer, drier weather, we decided to move up to La Saleta on Monday
and camp in the new living room, which was finished except for the
cork on the floor. We were leaving the following Saturday so time was
very short, and José and his workers had tried so valiantly to get the
house finished that maybe it would make them feel their efforts were
appreciated.

On Sunday the weather collapsed again. Wind and rain. The fire in
the old kitchen smoked dreadfully as gusts of wind blew the smoke

back down the chimney. We lit a fire in the new sitting room to try to warm and dry the room. It smoked too.

On Monday morning we packed up, bought a small stock of food and paid our bill at the Casa Rosita. The bill was absurdly small and we thought they had made a mistake. But no, the price they had given us (approximately sixteen shillings a day) was for both of us, not each. What a nice surprise!

Up at La Saleta we had to wait till evening to set up our camp beds. The men worked till dark every evening, and it was eight o'clock before José's boys had finished sweeping up and moving their clutter to leave us the room clear. We lit the fire, and José, the plumber, and Eugenio, who had just called in to see if we were all right, stood admiring it, thrilled like children round a Christmas tree and exclaiming with delight that the smoke and sparks went up the chimney so nicely. It would have been churlish to point out that the smoke came back down!

At last they all went away and we could settle down. I cooked our meal in the old kitchen the other side of the yard, by the light of our camping lantern and carried it across to our new fireside, avoiding the hazards, drain pipes, heaps of wet mixed cement, the big water barrel with a litter of broken tiles lying around it and the many bits and ends of rubbish that had been there for years. It rained.

We had electricity, but no plumbing yet, and it was not so romantic to go outside in the wet March weather as it had been in summer! We settled down to sleep by the flickering firelight. I woke several times in the night with a sense of strangeness, and in the morning the screeching of jays awoke us. It was cold and desolate to get up in the half-dark of the early morning and it was yet another wet day. However, after hot coffee, life seemed more cheerful and we set off in good time for Vigo.

The customs agent said yes, it was true that the Customs were going to release our things. But we must produce a bank guarantee. For how much? Ah, he did not know because the officer had not yet named a sum. Perhaps after lunch, say about half-past four.

Discouraged again, we went to meet Roderick who had a paper for us to sign. A bank guarantee? Yes, the bank manager could arrange that

1   *Arrival by road.*

2 & 3: La Saleta: neglected farm.

4 View of buildings from wood behind.

5 Don Severo's coat of arms.

6 *Village Post Office, 1970.*

7 *The water tank.*

8 Eugenio's house.

9 Eugenio's cork beehive.

10 La Saleta yard.

11 Restoration work begins.

12   Work under way.

13 Adjustment to front dooway.

14 Small farmhouse.

15 Farm cart.

but we would have to come back next day to complete the documentation. Perhaps we were nearing the end of this long-drawn-out affair.

On Wednesday we got up early to another gloomy, wet daybreak. We called at the bank in Pontevedra and the manager phoned Vigo to ask what sum of money was needed for the guarantee. To our exhausted frustration, the answer was that the Customs had not yet named a sum. "This afternoon perhaps, or *mañana*." With just two whole days left, our hopes were dwindling and we drove away to have lunch with the Manns, depressed and disappointed.

Roderick was upset by our news and phoned Vigo again, and now the agent said that perhaps he could get the answer about five-thirty that afternoon. As we would be well on our way back to La Saleta by then, Roderick promised to phone a message to the village exchange – if there was an answer. Meanwhile we must relax, and we spent a warm, happy day by their fireside, while the wind and rain swirled outside. By the time we left, we felt considerably revived and more able to cope with this game of snakes and ladders, or was it cat and mouse? At the exchange, yes, the message was waiting for us: 4,000 pesetas for the guarantee and 6,000 pesetas duty on the fridge.

Thursday morning the bank manager managed to settle the guarantee question. It was fortunate we had enough money available, which was only because of the delays to the building work. The documents were signed and now there was nothing more we could do. Just wait.

That day, Thursday, the building work was seriously held up by the pouring rain – all day. The painter could not get on, and the electricians had not appeared at all. Manuel, the plumber, was in trouble because he had been sure there was enough fall for the water to flow from the *mina* into the new cistern, and now it turned out there was not. We remembered that Antonio had queried Manuel's calculation in the beginning. So José, Manuel and the boy spent the afternoon deepening the already dug trench all the way, and in the cellar they were going to have to break up their newly concreted tank to make it several feet deeper. Poor José was dreadfully frustrated by this misfortune, and disappointed that he would not now be able to show us the house finished before we left. No matter that the cork for the floors had not arrived – they were not ready for it.

Now a decision faced us: should we ask Eugenio to unpack our furniture when it eventually arrived? We did not believe now that it would arrive before we left. We knew there were four packing cases, two of them huge and anyway it might not be possible to put them into a stable without first unpacking them. Eugenio worried about the mice again. We said, "Surely the house will be mouse-proof now. Don Antonio said it would be."

"No," said Eugenio. "Don Antonio is a townsman so he doesn't know. The mice have only gone away now because of the banging. They'll come back. They can come up the plumbers' pipes and they even eat mortar." He was right.

At nine o'clock that night there came a loud banging on the big front gate. The two men outside told us in loud shouts that a phone message had come to say that our furniture would be arriving next morning!

Next morning we waited. Robert and Eugenio went for a tour round the plants. There was the usual talk of money, vines, and the projected road improvement. We had lunch. No lorry appeared. I lay down on my bed to read my book.

Suddenly at four o'clock there was shouting and hooting. There on the green outside was a big red lorry with our cases under a tarpaulin. The driver, tubby and jovial, said he had got lost and was about to return to Vigo when he saw our GB car, and said to his mate, "That must be the place!"

Now how to get the cases off the lorry and into the yard? José came out to help and shouted to his team to come: "*Todos, todos!*" (Everyone, everyone!)

José, the tiler, two boys, the driver and his mate got to work. Someone was sent running to fetch Eugenio, but he was out.

It was a frightening business. The driver backed the lorry up close to the gateway. Then the men set up two strong planks from the lorry to the ground, sloping down into the entrance. Then they levered with slim pine poles, pushed from either side under the first big case and it slid heavily to the ground. Then, with a lot of heaving, they pushed two more pine poles under it and, after a series of huge pushes and shouts, it came in under the gateway, was turned sideways and shifted to the right-hand side so that the second box could be got in too. The two small boxes were no problem. The boys ran to and fro clearing building materials out of the way. Torrents of rain fell.

Now it was obvious that we would have to unpack the big cases where they were, as the gateway was completely blocked. But first Robert fetched a bottle of wine and everyone drank to celebrate the safe arrival and safe unloading, and then the lorry left. We stood and considered the situation. It was about six o'clock.

Once more José offered his help and I cannot imagine what we should have done without him. He got the cases open in a fraction of the time it would have taken us, and he helped unpack and carry. The men took the pieces of furniture into the house and I took the small things into the beehive room. Everything was under cover by the time dark and exhaustion overtook us. Now to have a meal and go to bed.

At this moment Celina appeared bringing us milk. She was delighted with our things and wanted to examine everything. "How beautiful it is," she said over and over again, and there was no way to hurry her tour of inspection, the bathroom, the furniture, the fireplace—"Oh, how beautiful!"

"What are you going to do about the two little rooms at the front? And the caretakers' kitchen?" she asked. And then, most unanswerable of all: "Why do you need so much house?"

And so next morning we were packed by nine o'clock, said the last goodbyes and drove off, stopping at the telephone exchange to phone Roderick with the good news and to say thank you. Then we drove away southwards, across the frontier and down the Portuguese coast road in sheets of rain and wild buffeting winds. From the road we caught glimpses of mountainous Atlantic waves, the mud-coloured rivers ran full, and little streams rushed along beside and across the roadway. In the evening we stopped at a warm hotel and had hot baths, and a first-class dinner, and enjoyed, as never before, a comfortable, dry and clean night. Next day we sailed from Lisbon for England.

10

Summer and sun

"Val máis fume da miña casiña que lume da miña veciña." (Gallego saying)
The smoke of my little house is worth more than my neighbour's fire.

When we arrived in July 1969 there was beautiful hot sunshine. There was our newly remade little house, with electric light and running water, doors and windows that opened and shut. Inside, the white paint on the walls brought out the rich grey tones of the granite of the door and window surrounds and of the *lareira*. The house was clean and crisp and cool, in restful contrast to the dazzling sunshine outside. We wiped the green mould off the furniture and arranged it. Now we had real beds, armchairs, a dining table and chairs. We unpacked the things Eugenio had hung up in sacks from the beams in the beehive room. We cleared the worst weeds and remains of builders' rubble from the yard and from the little garden outside the new sitting-room French window. We struggled with the eccentricities of the WC flush, a complicated contraption with many small screws and basically unreliable. (It gave trouble from time to time for the next twenty-five years, until a visiting engineer-tenant made a small part on his return to England, and the following tenant, also an engineer, fixed it!) Now we enjoyed a family holiday.

One great pleasure was to go to the twice-monthly market in the village, famous in the area. It was a bigger affair than we had realised. It had been held on the 9th and 24th of each month since 1895 at least. It made no difference if the date fell on a Sunday, or even on Good Friday; indeed Sunday markets were best, people were freer to dally, gossiping, bargaining, buying and selling, and courting. It was the heart of social life in the countryside and people came from miles around. Now, however, much of the flavour has gone, because a new livestock market with modern installations has been built a little way away, much more hygienic and efficient no doubt, but less picturesque and entertaining.

As we walked down the hill to the market place, we fell in with more and more people going the same way, some leading a cow or two, a sheep or a goat, others carrying hens or a basket of eggs, fruit or vegetables. Carts, cars, vans and lorries jammed the approach roads. We found the market in full swing under the plane trees of the unpaved square. A large part of the square was given over to livestock, mainly cows, and there, owners and animals stood in a tightly packed mass, patiently waiting. There was plenty of talking and shouting while the animals fidgeted, nudged each other and pissed. The cows had full udders, to show their value, and towards the end of the morning if the animal was not sold, some milk would have to be let out to ease the pressure. All around the animals and over on the other side of the square, were tables set up with fruit, vegetables, cheeses, breads made from rye, maize or wheat. There were women standing to one side, selling onions, greens for planting, sacks of haricot beans, or eggs by the dozen. Agricultural implements, rope and baskets were being sold from a van and there were stalls with pots and pans, plastics, crockery, textiles, clothing and shoes. A small corner of the square was paved and roofed, and here meat and fish were sold, the fish from long concrete slabs running down the centre of the building and the meat from little shops built in around the walls.

Then there was the octopus seller, who travelled from market to market with a big cauldron in which the octopus was boiled over an open fire. Once cooked, it was fished out of the water, cut up into small pieces with scissors and served on wooden platters, well seasoned with vinegar, salt and pepper. The customers then adjourned to the nearest bar to eat the tasty, chewy pink fingers accompanied by hunks of bread and washed down by the sour local red wine.

There was a *churros* stall too. *Churros* are small fingers made of a flour and water paste forced through a giant mincing machine and fried in boiling oil. You buy ten or twenty and they are served to you in a twist of paper sprinkled with sugar. The best ones we knew were sold down on the water front of the nearest port, by an old crone in a dirty, ramshackle shack, but unfortunately the municipality cleaned up the area and threw away shack and old dame, replacing them by a neat hut and a middle-aged man, whose *churros* were not in the same class.

The market was extremely noisy. In Galicia, buying and selling is argumentative and peasant voices loud. Cows moo and sheep baa. Some vendors had loudspeakers to broadcast their wares, or radios blaring out music.

Past midday, the stalls packed up and the populace set out homeward or adjourned to the bar leaving their livestock tied up outside or loaded into the cow-bus ready to go home.

Eugenio and his friends went to cattle markets in towns and villages in perhaps a radius of thirty miles. They travelled by cow-bus – I don't know what else to call it. It was a vehicle the size of a van. In the front there were seats for about six passengers in two rows, and, behind a partition, an enclosure for about ten cows. Privately owned, the charges were per person and per cow. Getting the cows in and out, up or down a wooden ramp was not an easy job. Passing drivers beware: cows might suddenly rush down the ramp and into the road.

Trading in cows to Eugenio was what trading in stocks and shares is to a capitalist, and his hobby as well. He was a good judge of a cow and a gifted handler, qualities he inherited from his father. He used to buy one or two at a time, feed them up and sell them again when they were in peak condition and prices high.

He told me about payment: "When one sells a cow, maybe one doesn't get paid till next market day, unless the cow is bought by the slaughterhouse – they pay at once. A private buyer never pays all the money at once, he pays perhaps half, and the balance after a month if the cow is healthy and well behaved. If not, he returns the animal and should be refunded his money. Once I didn't get it. I bought a cow which turned out to be a bad one, so I took her back to her previous owner who turned very nasty and went for me with his pitchfork.

Fortunately a friend of mine appeared just then and I could make my escape – quick! I was lucky that time though. I took the cow to Vigo and sold her, put the money in my pocket and came back to the village before the new owner realised the cow was a bad one."

Eugenio told me another story about a cow he had difficulty in disposing of. Maybe it was the same one. She was pale coloured and well known to be bad, so he painted her brown, but unfortunately it rained and the colour washed off, so that plan failed.

Some years later I took my ninety-year-old father to the market, and he wandered precariously among the animals, delighted to enjoy, once again, the sights, sound and smells of his childhood in Ireland.

When our family's holiday came to an end, we saw them off on the night train to Madrid, and Robert and I had to plan ahead. We planned to return in February, this time to settle down to live at La Saleta, so there were matters to settle. We asked Eugenio if he could find a gardener to work for us. We knew we would not find anyone who knew anything about gardening, but perhaps we could find a young man who would be willing to learn? Eugenio said it would be difficult because all the young men went away to work abroad and earned lots of money, and those few who stayed at home were no good. He leaned on his spade to demonstrate how anyone from the next village would work. We asked about his son-in-law, Ernesto, and Eugenio thought a minute and said just possibly. Ernesto had old parents and an old uncle, a wife and small child and a grandmother, so he couldn't go abroad; he had a small farm, but maybe his father and his wife could look after it; he lived about three miles away.

A few days later Eugenio brought Ernesto to see us. We explained that we wanted someone to work one day a week during the following winter months and then full-time when we came to settle next February. Both men were mystified about what we planned to do, as making a pleasure garden was entirely beyond their range of ideas. To grow flowers for the market, now that would be profitable, or vegetables, or even to plant a fruit orchard. But a garden? A park? What for?

In the south of Spain there is a long-established tradition of making gardens and flowery patios, a tradition brought by the Arabs who were particularly fond of courtyards with fountains and shady trees. In

Spanish towns there are always pot plants on balconies or beside the front door, and every little town bigger than a village, has its town square with trees, benches, and a few formal flowerbeds. Aristocrats' palaces have gardens and pleasure parks in all parts of Spain, and in Galicia the only gardens there are belong to *pazos* and modern town houses. However, since the countryside had suffered from poverty for centuries, it is understandable that the idea was strange.

We had a general garden plan, drawn up for us by a garden designer in England from photographs and measurements, and we showed it to Eugenio and Ernesto, who gazed at it bewildered, and I do not think it meant anything to them at all. Suddenly Eugenio pointed to one of the little sketches around the plan which showed imaginary vistas or corners of the garden-to-be.

"Those are trees," he said, surprised. "That is for *mañana*. There is nothing like that there today."

Ernesto said he would think about our suggestion, discuss it with his wife and come back to see us in a few days. Two days later he came again, once more escorted by Eugenio, and we all sat down round the table and drank wine, talking of the weather, the crops and various other matters. More relevantly than perhaps he knew, Eugenio gave us a lecture on learning how to bargain. He did not even buy a suit in Pontevedra, he said, without getting the price reduced. Coming to the point, at last, Robert put the question: what did Ernesto think?

"Well," said Ernesto, "I think Don Robert is offering very little money."

The offer had been 4,800 pesetas a month. How much did he want then? Ernesto said 7,000. Robert did some sums on a scrap of paper and said that was too much, say 6,000. Ernesto said no. Robert said, "What a pity." There was a silence, and then Eugenio observed conversationally that it had nothing to do with him. More silence. They got up to go.

"6,500," said Ernesto, and Robert agreed.

As we cleared up and prepared to leave, it seemed strange to think that, next time we came, it would be to stay. How would it turn out? And I wondered what would become of our relationship with Eugenio and Celina when we actually lived there. From the first they had given us a straightforward, person-to-person friendship, but our standard of living and our personal possessions were those of another world. We came from another world. This would be even more obvious when we came to build a new house, as we intended to do. Could they possibly not resent our relative wealth?

Our last evening we tried to pay for the milk we had had from Eugenio's farm. It was not the first attempt by any means. Celina thrust the money back into my hands and said fiercely, "If you must pay for the milk, then goodbye friendship." Fortunately, however, we did get them to agree that once we were living permanently at La Saleta, we should pay for our milk.

"If we can supply you," said Eugenio. "If not, we shall have to find someone trustworthy – some of them add water to the milk, you know."

11

Rosa Varela's vines

"Falar, ben falas! Máis a verdade non parece." (Gallego saying)
Talk, you talk well! But it does not seem the truth.

I have left aside one matter from the previous chapter, which caused us considerable bother that summer of 1969, and which deserves a chapter to itself.

During our February visit that year, Robert had written to a chemical firm about weed killers and spraying equipment, and two agricultural experts visited us. They could supply a suitable weed killer, they said, and if we could find two men to work for us for about ten days on spraying, they would send someone to show them how to do it. So we asked Eugenio who said he would do it himself and find another man to help him.

The first warning of trouble came in a letter we received from Eugenio in June. It was an incoherent letter and we did not fully understand it. It was difficult for Eugenio to write about anything complicated, and he was upset when he wrote it. As I understood it later, this is what the letter said – with some added punctuation: "…the *señores* of the chemical firm came the second time to bring me some more spray for the weeds in May and it was raining for a long time and when the weather improved a bit I went on spraying as they had shown me. But now it is very hot and there is a north wind and the nearest vines are getting infected and yours too and the vines at the bottom which belong to Rosa are almost all dried up. She came twice to my house. I told her it was not the spray. The neighbours all say it was, because the smell is very strong in the heat and it is said that plants breathe like everything else. I tested it in my *finca* to see if it was that and I infected my vines, all the ones which were near, so for the moment, until you come, I am not spraying any more because all the neighbours are protesting. I wrote to the firm to come and look..."

Poor Eugenio! We answered that we hoped that the chemical firm's experts had come to look and to tell him what to do. If there was damage to other people's vines we would talk about it when we came.

On 12th July, Eugenio wrote again: "...about the spray, well, the *señores* of the chemical firm came and told me it was the spray in the heat. I wanted to take them to see the owner of the vineyard but they would not go and they told me to tell her that they were sending me something (to cure it) but she would not have it and she complained to the *Hermandad.* I don't know what is to be done. When you come we'll talk about it...there isn't any wine this year." (He meant that there were very few grapes on anyone's vines.)

As soon as we arrived Eugenio told us all about it and the gist of the matter was this: Rosa Varela owned a tiny vineyard adjacent to the bottom of our land. She had lodged a formal complaint with the *Hermandad* (a state-controlled farmers' union) and in due course we might have to answer with our side of the case. In the meanwhile, Eugenio thought that the *Hermandad* might decide not to pursue the matter, so he strongly advised that we do nothing at all unless asked, and even then we should deny responsibility, at least to begin with, because if we paid up, all the neighbours around would try it on, and as it was a hopelessly bad grape year, they would all like to say that their vines had withered from breathing our noxious spray. In fact, there were no grapes even on perfectly healthy vines that year.

We could see for ourselves that it was true that some vines in Rosa's little vineyard had died and that others were poorly. She lived across the valley and we had never met her. Fortunately, it was clearly true that other neighbours had suffered no damage because none of their vineyards were adjacent to our land.

It was only later that we were able to fill in the details of this dispute. Undoubtedly there had been a tremendous dust-up between Eugenio and Rosa and that unpardonable things had been said, among them that she was the daughter of a ***** or so I supposed. However, Eugenio had good reason to call her stupid when she refused to try the remedy supplied by the chemical firm. Or had she a better plan in mind?

In the ordinary way small local disputes were referred to the village *Juez de la paz* (Justice of the peace), who was not a lawyer but a respected villager and had power to deal with disputes and petty crime. More serious matters were referred to the district magistrate in a nearby town. In his court it was necessary, in fact if not in theory, to employ a lawyer to represent one.

We were told about an interesting quarrel between one of our acquaintances, Regina, and her neighbour with whom she shared a washing place. The neighbour accused Regina of stealing a pair of knickers and Regina slapped her in the face. The neighbour then lodged a complaint with the district magistrate saying she had been ill for some days after being hit. Both parties had to appear before the magistrate and Regina wanted to speak for herself, but the magistrate insisted that she must have a lawyer because the other woman had. In the end the matter was settled by the payment of a small fine.

I was told that litigation used to be something of a Galician's hobby. In the countryside there was plenty to quarrel about: the plots of land were sometimes so small that a turning plough might cross the boundary and a cow might eat the neighbour's grass; access to one person's field could be across another's land, and there were seldom clear markers between strips of woodland. Anyway whose tree was it which grew exactly on the boundary? Nowadays it is increasingly realised that it is not worthwhile having legal disputes about trifles.

In the case of Rosa Varela's vines, presumably she took her complaint to the *Hermandad* because a lawyer would not be needed. The secretary of the *Hermandad* sent us an urgent message to come. We went, accompanied by Eugenio, and sat down in the little office and the secretary showed us the typewritten complaint: our spray had killed a lot of vines and caused a complete lack of grapes this year. We pointed out that this was untrue: only a few vines had been damaged and some of those were going to recover, and that there were no grapes on anyone's vines anyway. Eugenio and the secretary agreed, but said that all complaints started out with untruths. We said that we were prepared to pay reasonable compensation for the actual damage, and the secretary said that obviously we did not want to pay for vines which were going to recover; he would appoint two independent villagers to go and assess the damage and let us know how much they said.

A week later we got another message asking us to come to the office to meet Rosa Varela, but, as she did not appear, a definite appointment was made for twelve o'clock the following day. Before we left the office, the secretary gave us a copy of the estimate of the damage she had brought him, a formal statement drawn up by a "doctor of agriculture". There were three headings:

1. Loss of the whole wine crop in the vineyard for this season.
2. Probable loss of the crop to be expected on 78 vines next year.
3. Replacement of 56 dead vines. Total damage: 10,000 pesetas
   – about £60 in those days.

We studied this document carefully and consulted Eugenio, who explained that the two village assessors had refused to make an estimate because, they said, we should have to send for an expert ourselves and their valuation might be quite wrong, which would be embarrassing for them. They knew how to decide the value of one stolen cow or one damaged pine tree, but this was too big a matter. Eugenio also told us that the secretary of the *Hermandad* had run after him down the road to tell him to be sure to tell us, off the cuff, that there was no hurry to pay.

"I suppose the doctor of agriculture isn't a relation of Rosa's?" I ventured to ask.

"No," answered Eugenio. "He's a friend of her husband's."

Next morning we duly reported to the office, where Rosa was waiting. A large red-faced woman, she greeted us with great affability and a wide toothless smile and ushered us inside. She did not want to quarrel with us, she assured us, but Eugenio did get so angry! We suspected a long-standing animosity.

The interview went like this: Robert started by saying that we were not prepared to discuss such a high price and were going to consult our own expert. The secretary nodded cautious approval.

Rosa said she wanted the matter settled before we went away again, and Robert answered that we had already written to our expert, and asked her permission to take him into her vineyard when he arrived.

She said that of course she was not going to prejudice the outcome, but her expert was a very learned expert. Robert answered, as best he could, that other learned experts might have other opinions, at which the secretary laughed loudly. Then we said we were sorry about her vines and got up and left.

At the time I thought it was a great pity that we had got into this kind of difficulty so soon, but, in retrospect, I think perhaps it did us good. We had been obliged to come down from our Mount Olympus and grapple with a personal and practical problem concerning the villagers. Possibly they understood us better as a result.

A few days later, *Señor* A and *Señor* M came from the chemical firm. Yes, they said, this kind of accident happened quite often. The spray vaporises very fast in hot weather, and they had not noticed that little vineyard below the wall there, or they would have warned Eugenio. At this stage they refused to send a message to Rosa to come because they wanted to have a careful and quiet look first. *Señor* A examined the vines carefully and worked out a rough estimate of the damage. The first point on her document was certainly disputable but nevertheless he estimated the damage at about 8,000 pesetas. He would work it out in detail in his office and return the following Monday bringing us a suitably imposing document setting out his opinion, and signed with his full name and qualifications. Then, if we insisted, we could ask Rosa to come and meet him.

It was interesting that her figure had not been so widely exaggerated as we had supposed, and it was therefore no wonder that the village assessors had been unwilling to suggest a figure, and that she was pressing for payment. It would be a big sum of money to her, and new vines would have to be planted early in the following spring.

So, on Monday, our experts returned with a splendidly impressive document. Reluctantly they came down to the vineyard to meet Rosa who was waiting. *Señor* A was a courteous, rather gentle man, but he played his part well when it came to the point, though it was certainly hard work. He read through his estimate, stubbornly reiterating his points while Rosa ranted and raged at him. While we could not understand much of what she said, I did catch that she wanted compensation not only for the vines but also for Eugenio's insults! After a time, *Señor* A turned to us and, speaking very slowly and carefully, explained that she would accept his figure. We were astonished! She had shown no signs, that we had seen, of accepting anything.

Robert had enough money in the house to settle at once and asked whether we needed to go to the *Hermandad* office to pay? No, anywhere would do, and so now, Rosa all smiles, we went up to the house and while *Señor* A typed out a form of receipt with two copies, Robert fetched wine and *Señor* M engaged Rosa successfully in conversation, a good deal of which was about her spectacular quarrel with Eugenio.

The money was handed over, Rosa signed the receipt and the two expects signed as witnesses. We had a glass of wine all round and then the difficulty was to bring the party to an end, as Rosa would have been happy to stay for hours drinking wine and asking about everyone's families. Gradually we eased her out of the door and across the yard, *Señor* A murmuring in my ear that if we thought the firm had a responsibility, because they had not warned Eugenio of the dangers in hot weather, they would pay half the damage – which they did later. They gave Rosa a lift to the village and we took the receipt to the *Hermandad*. Matter settled.

Years passed and Rosa never replaced the dead vines. Many of the sick and apparently dead ones recovered, and then the whole field turned into a bramble thicket. Whenever I met her she greeted me as a long-lost friend, but Eugenio still growled that she was a *burra* (a she-donkey), and, whatever may have been the morals of Rosa or her mother, years later I found out from the parish records that her grandmother was probably of doubtful virtue.

12

Settling down

"Onde unha porta se pecha, outra se abre." (Gallego saying)
Where one door shuts, another opens.

In Galicia our peasant neighbours would have considered it unthinkable to sell their houses and land and go away, that is unless forced by financial necessity. Innumerable Galicians have emigrated in the past, with great heartbreak, mainly to South America, and more recently to Northern Europe.

But they did not sell their properties, but left them in the care of their families who remained, and they left with the dream that, one day, they would return, rich, to their ancestral homes. Sometimes they did.

Our case was very different. We expected to visit England and our families and friends often, and we expected them to visit us. We were bringing our belongings with us, and in our culture the idea of changing residence and way of life is not strange. We felt great excitement and stimulus about setting out on this new chosen life, but all the same I found breaking up our English home very painful. To me, home is more than a house, its rooms, its furnishings – it is in some way part of me. Robert seemed less affected.

Three days before we left, my father fell ill and was taken into hospital. His condition, though serious, was not so grave as to justify delaying our departure, but it added another strand to my anguish. We were both very tired indeed by the time we got ourselves, Morris car, and Land Rover towing trailer, on to the ferry from Southampton to Bilbao on 16th February 1970. I felt as if I had been torn apart.

Our furniture, for the new house we planned to build, was being professionally packed and was to be sent after us as soon as the formalities could be completed. What we had with us in the tightly packed, overloaded cars, was a selection of small domestic equipment, house linen and blankets, clothes, gardening tools, et cetera, that is, the things we should need at once. The trailer was full of plants.

The ship docked punctually, early on the morning of the 18th and we were off and away, sooner than we had ever hoped. In the grey, early morning light, the queue of cars moved steadily through passport control, and what a relief it was that there was no sign of any customs officials who might stop and search such heavily laden cars. All manner of things were dutiable or forbidden entry in those days.

As we drove westwards, in the crisp sparkling weather, our spirits rose steadily, on and on westwards, towards the future.

We arrived at La Saleta late in the afternoon of the 19th to find that Celina and her daughter had opened up and swept and dusted the house for us, and Ernesto had tidied up the yards, clearing away the rubbish and builders' rubble – a warm welcome and a great improvement. It took ages to unpack the cars: it was difficult to imagine how so much could have been got into them. Eugenio and Celina helped, exclaiming at our mountain of possessions, and then went away to milk their cows and we settled down for the evening.

We felt frozen. We lit the fire, which smoked, and the butane gas heater, and hung our sheets and blankets in front, turning them round and round as the steam rose from them, and we were glad to have electric blankets for our beds. The old house was always cold in winter because of the thick stone walls, and because the windows had no frames. Also we were accustomed to central heating. I felt cold for several days, cold and tired and disoriented, unable to stand up to the difficulties that confronted us. Robert set to work, totally concentrated on caring for his plants.

Our fatigue began to wear off gradually; we slept wonderfully and the house began to warm up; the fire stopped smoking and the evenings were really cosy with the shutters closed and the curtains drawn. Some sort of rhythm of life began to be established.

"How do you feel about it?" Roderick asked me when he and Ana came over to lunch one of those early days.

I could only reply that it was too soon to answer. I felt dazed and it was as much as I could do to face up to the day-to-day problems of living, without trying to see further ahead.

At once, there were problems with the electricity supply and the water pump. The house water was pumped up from the tank in the cellar floor, automatically when a tap was opened, but when we arrived the automatic switch was not working. We could only get water by going down to the cellar and operating the switch by hand. We were longing for hot baths but as the water was heated by passing at an even speed through a geyser, hot water seemed impractical. We sent an urgent message to Lauriano, the Pontevedra electrician who had installed the pump. Four days later we sent a second message.

During the following two weeks:

♦ Lauriano came twice and repaired the automatic mechanism.
♦ The whole electricity supply failed three times because the main fuse blew.
♦ The village electrician mended it twice and the third time put in a new bigger meter.
♦ This proved too much for the pump automatic which failed again.
♦ And then, Lauriano, very grim faced, put a whole new automatic mechanism into the pump, which worked happily ever after.

Saturday, 13th March. Bath night! And we could wash our clothes too, most conveniently in the bath. Drying though, was more difficult as the air in Galicia is very damp in winter. I hung up a line in one of the outhouses but it could take a week for things to dry and then they had to be finished off on a towel horse by the fire when we went to bed. Clean clothes were therefore something of a luxury until spring came.

Shopping proved surprisingly difficult. When we were on holiday we had bought food from day to day, but now I wanted to cater in an organised way, and I planned to go to Pontevedra only once a week to stock up. Two days after our arrival I went to the Pontevedra market. It was absolute bedlam, the noise and bustle altogether more than I could cope with. I was only able to choose the nearest fish and a piece of meat, almost at random, and then I fled. It was weeks before I learnt to market reasonably efficiently. Sometimes I was clear-headed and competent, but other days all the fish looked strange and menacing, odd shapes and colours. Occasionally, feeling reckless, I bought strange sea monsters only to realise, when I got home, that I had no idea what to do with them. Once I had to consult the plumber.

Pontevedra market was then an ugly, grey stone building beside the river. In winter it was very cold. Inside, the ground floor was laid out with rows of stands for fish, each with a centre passageway where the sellers stood and shouted and argued and cursed in traditional fishwife fashion. They were all women, most of them elderly and stout. You were expected to bargain for your fish, which was beyond me since I found it difficult enough to choose, decide how much I wanted and calculate the cost. In the long run, my obvious inadequacy brought its own benefits, as some of the nicer fishwives came to know me and to feel ashamed of doing me down, and so began to throw in an extra fish, "For you, *señora!*" I was interested to notice too that, although no doubt they sometimes charged me too much, they were scrupulously careful to give correct change and to make sure that I understood that they had.

Built in around the inside walls of the building were small butchers' shops. Here it was easier to make one's voice heard and to negotiate, as the butchers, male and female, were a quieter type of person. One butcher-lady asked me:

"Are you from the Russian circus, *señora?* I can see you are not from here!"

Two open squares were occupied by flower sellers, their flowers a blaze of colour, especially on Saturdays and before feast days. Upstairs were fruit and vegetable stalls, with an impressive array of colourful produce, and around the walls small grocers' shops and various kinds of specialists, selling potatoes, eggs, dried beans and grains, strings of sausages of all shapes and sizes, cheeses and breads. A tough, noisy, vigorously cut-throat world.

The town housewife expected to go to market every morning, so between about ten and eleven-thirty was rush-hour as the jostling crowd of women with bags and baskets pushed their way round, arguing about everything. They met their friends too, and held long, shouted conversations in the aisles. From time to time, new supplies of fish were carried in from lorries, a loud bell was rung, and some of the fishwives left their posts to go off and haggle with the suppliers just inside the doorway. They carried the fish to their stands in baskets on their heads, or else it was brought by tough old hags with small barrows, pushing through the crowd shouting, "C*uidao…cuidao…cuidao!*" (Look out! Look out!) It was up to the public to mind their shins, and to avoid being knocked over by whole carcasses of meat on men's shoulders. Blind sellers of lottery tickets were another hazard. They pushed their unseeing way through the shoppers with their cry of "*tres iguales*" (three equal ones). I never discovered three equal what?

Everywhere one only got served by asserting oneself, as queuing was not a local custom. To be fair though, the foreigner or obvious stranger got served first and given the best attention. Very soon I realised that I did not know how to say, "It's my turn now," and was therefore poorly equipped to assert myself. A Spanish friend taught me the idiomatic phrase I needed and I tried it out. The effect was startling! The other customers stopped their pushing to stare at me, as surprised as if a fish on the slab had protested.

In shops the procedure was different, as the assistant would ask everyone waiting what they wanted. The most determined customer then shoved her way to the front, maybe announcing that her bus was just about to leave, and by the time she was disposed of, the assistant had forgotten who he was going to serve and started all over again. Patience and stamina were required but it could be entertaining, with much gossip and jokes shared. Now thirty years later, supermarkets have made shopping easier, but much of the old flavour has been lost.

The weather that spring was fine and sunny but with a very cold wind. We both got chilblains, but it was warm enough to sit outside many afternoons. My fatigue wore off slowly and I deliberately did not try to hurry my adjustment. In any case the simple life is very time-consuming.

Ernesto started daily work immediately we arrived. The first morning I looked out of the window and saw it was raining, and there down the field was Ernesto, digging with one hand while he held his umbrella over his head with the other. I went to tell him that there was no sense in getting wet like that, and he answered sadly that he had asked Don Roberto whether he should come on wet days and Don Roberto had said yes. I assured him that Don Roberto did not intend him to get soaked and that there were plenty of jobs under cover for wet days, so he spent the rest of that day clearing out an old stable to make a storeroom. This little episode was a warning to us of how easily misunderstandings could arise because Ernesto's whole experience was so different from ours. Also it illustrates a difficulty that was always with us: the education, in its widest sense, of the country people had not taught them to think for themselves. On their own farms, the year's work was laid down by long tradition, and in their dealings with the Church and State they had to obey without questioning, so as employees, they did exactly what they were told, no more, no less. If the circumstances changed, then it was the employer's business to think.

At the end of that day, Ernesto called us to admire the beautiful clean state of the stable and asked whether Don Roberto was satisfied with his work. Robert said yes, indeed, but was he satisfied? Ernesto then explained that he had asked because he wanted to buy a small motor bicycle, as he found the ride to work too far on his push bike. Four years later, he was able to buy a small second-hand car, and in twenty years, his whole standard of living had changed, and with it his confidence and his status in his community.

Eugenio and Celina were fascinated by our possessions. Robert demonstrated how the electric toaster worked and they jumped out of their skins when it popped up. Their curiosity was frank and unbounded and sometimes embarrassing but I never felt it was envious or hostile. We tried to answer them directly and sincerely. Celina was worried: where would we be buried when we died? Here or back in England? We said that as we were not Catholics it would have to be the garden or the hillside surely? Celina said no, she thought that if we made friends with Don Maximino, the priest, he would put us in his graveyard.

They were worried too about how sad it would be for us as we grew old, without our families living around us. Their two sons had gone away to Brazil because there was no livelihood for them on the farm, and poor opportunities elsewhere around, and they would probably never come back. "But, rich people like you should not have this trouble." We found it difficult to explain to them that families in England nowadays seldom live all in the same village or neighbourhood, and that it was precisely because we were well-to-do that we would be able to go to England quite often.

"How curious it is," said Eugenio. "You have come to live here in the country and you say you like the peace and quiet. But I'm tired of the country. I should like to live on the edge of a town and then I should be able to go and have coffee in cafés with my friends."

We asked if he had ever been away from Galicia.

"Oh yes," he said. "I went to the war – you know that war we had. We went right away over the mountains and it was terrible – nothing good to eat at all. After the war I tried working in a mine in Asturias, but that was terrible too. I couldn't bear to go tunnelling in the ground. I'm a man, not a mole – so I worked as watchman at the top. But that was too dull, I couldn't stand that, so I came home again, back to the *finca*."

Robert asked Eugenio where we could buy a barrel of wine, and he found a friend, a cattle dealer, with some wine to sell, and he took us to taste it. On arrival at the house we were taken down to the wine cellar. There were four big barrels, lying horizontally, and a little wine was drawn into small white basins in turn from each barrel so we could taste one after another. I was afraid that we would not be able to detect any difference between them, but luckily Robert and I agreed that the wine in the first barrel was best. There were interruptions: by the village idiot who emptied one basin when no one was looking, and by an inquisitive sheep who kept joining the party and having to be shooed away. Eugenio held back tactfully while we tasted and then came forward and tasted. We were glad indeed when he gave his judgement: that the first barrel was the best, the most *amoroso*, (loving). A price was named and we agreed to come back another day to fetch our wine.

A big barrel, a *pipa*, holds five hundred and twenty-two litres and we decided we wanted half a *pipa*, so we bought a small barrel on our way home from a bar. The following Sunday we set off to fetch our wine. Once more the little basins were brought out and we tasted the wine again to make sure we still liked it. Did we want our wine measured out into our barrel with a measuring jug, or should they siphon it in with a rubber tube? The latter method seemed simpler and quicker, but then no suitable tube could be found, so they tied two thin ones together, but then discovered that one was too short because, our host explained, his son had taken a piece to siphon petrol into his car. A bigger and longer tube was borrowed and one end was tied to a stick that they pushed through the hole in the barrel. Our host then put his head over a basin, gave a good suck at the other end, pinched the end with his finger and thumb as soon as the wine began to flow through, and thrust it into the small hole in the top of our barrel.

Filling our barrel took a long time, so we were taken to admire the animals: three cows, two little calves, a fine big horse and three elegant and quiet dogs such as are seldom found on these farms. Then wine glasses were brought, and bread and slices of *chorizo* (sausage), and our hosts invited us to try their white wine, which we found crisp and tangy. Eventually our barrel was full, and after much tapping and banging and adding a little more from the jug, it was judged absolutely full, and they pushed in the cork, which was wrapped up in a piece of sacking and a piece of white rag. Some neighbours had to be fetched to help lift the heavy barrel up into the Land Rover and wedge it in with sticks and stones. Then Robert got out his wallet to pay.

"No hurry," said our host. "Another day."

We found it odd that no one seemed in a hurry to be paid and we could only suppose it was a matter of pride: no one wanted to seem to need the money. Nor had there been any bargaining about the price. On the way over, Eugenio had explained to us that bargaining was for the market place but that, in a private house transaction, a price was a price. Maybe, but I think myself that this was not strictly true, but rather that he and his friend had already worked out the price and agreed it at the previous day's market. In later years we went out on several such wine-buying expeditions, generally with Eugenio as our guide and mentor, and there was certainly discussion about the price, if not real bargaining as a Galician would understand it. It would take a seller a long time to name his price; first one had to discuss the weather, the harvest, the welfare and whereabouts of families; one had to agree that life was getting very expensive nowadays. The seller then talked about the cost of wine in bars, and then that he heard that his neighbour sold a barrel last week for a high price because there was such a shortage of good wine that year. Buyer and seller then agreed that one could not be too careful about the quality. The buyer should then say that he heard that some other neighbour had some very good wine to sell, and that he could only afford to pay so much. In the end, the deal completed, the buyer would be asked into the house to have a drink of the best home wine served with bread and *chorizo*.

We bought rough red wine that first time and we paid seventeen and a half pesetas a litre – about twelve old pence in those days. The local red wine is acid because there is not enough sun in the late summer to ripen the grapes sufficiently, but the people like it that way and consider that Castilian wine has no taste – watery stuff, they say, and go on to assure you that those Castilians put water in it anyway, in order to make it go further.

The local white wines are very much better quality. There are two kinds: *Catalán* and *Albariño*, the latter worth twice as much as the former. *Albariño* is the only named, export quality wine produced in the area, and not a great quantity was then produced, partly because the grapes need a lot more spraying than the white *Catalán* grapes and also because they only grow well in certain limited areas. Year by year though, the market for *Albariño* has soared, and every year more is produced and exported.

The *Albariño* grape was brought to Galicia by the Benedictine monks from Cluny in the twelfth century. They played an important part in organising and publicising the pilgrimage to the putative tomb of Saint James in Santiago de Compostela, and they founded monasteries and hospices all along that pilgrim road. What could be more natural than that they should have brought their best grapes with them?

On 22nd March, barely a month after our arrival, I was sent for urgently from England because my father was dangerously ill. It was nearly a month before I returned, during which time María-Ester, Celina's daughter, had come across twice a day to cook, most inadequately, for Robert. I arrived back on a cold wet day in April, very tired and distressed as I thought, wrongly as it turned out, that I had said goodbye to my father for ever. But, yes, I did feel I had come home.

13

Formalities

"Con paciencia e con saliva, non hai cousa que non se consiga."
(Gallego saying)
With patience and saliva there is nothing one cannot manage.

Now it was full springtime and I returned from England to find the
oaks bursting into leaf, grey-green against the dark mass of the pines;
fruit blossom was out in fields, and orchards; by the roadsides bloomed
innumerable wild flowers, and around our land were big clumps of bright
blue lithospermums. The tips of the pine branches held up an abundance
of pinky-red flowers, which, from a distance looked like candles. They
shed a greeny-yellow pollen during the two or three weeks of their
flowering season, which got into and onto everything, and made wearing
contact lenses intolerable.

The sun shone, the air warmed up, and lizards of all sizes came out
to bask on the walls. Ernesto found several small snakes in the rough
grass. Suddenly, one night, the frogs set up their croaking and the crickets
their chirrup.

We had to make a start almost at once on what was to be a long,
long struggle to get, and keep, our papers in order. At the time I did not
realise what a struggle it was going to be, nor that it was one that was
never ended.

Gradually we came to know that it was a hard basic fact of life in
Galicia that we could not deal with any official business without a
disproportionate amount of wear and tear. Try as we would, we did not

really understand the rules, partly due to inadequate Spanish, but more because of the difference in thinking and attitudes of another country's bureaucracy, developed in the course of centuries. I suppose that foreigners living in England feel this same bafflement when confronted by English rules and regulations.

Our difficulties over importing the furniture for the old house had taught us to tread carefully where the Customs were concerned. Now we had a much bigger consignment to come, to furnish the new house we planned to have built. But first we had to get ourselves residence permits, first temporary for three months, and then permanent. For this we had to collect: a paper from the British consulate; a paper from the Ministry of Labour saying that we were not employed in Spain nor intending to be; a document from our local *Ayuntamiento* signed by two guarantors; four photos and two official stamps, and finally a document from our nearest *Guardia Civil*, where we had to fill in huge forms and provide thumb prints. Then the application could go to Madrid.

As for the furniture, we also needed a detailed list of every item in both languages, and the to and fro of correspondence lasted all summer, held up by a strike of the ferry which was to bring our things, and the lack of some paper which we should have had before leaving England, which our son managed to obtain by going personally to the Spanish Embassy in London. Finally, early in September, one morning at nine a.m., three twenty-foot containers arrived on two lorries, which had driven the four hundred and fifty miles from Bilbao the previous day and hoped to get back there that same night. We had had no warning and we had an exhausting scramble to unload and stow everything under cover in the outhouses before nightfall, helped by Ernesto and by Eugenio and his family. It was six months since we had seen our possessions disappearing into furniture vans outside our English home.

Some of the tangles of business led round and round in circles. When we applied for Spanish driving licences we needed medical certificates, a paper from Madrid to say we had no criminal records, and a letter from the *Guardia Civil*, which we had visited so recently. However, they could not give it to us until our residence permits came through.

Then we discovered we would have to take a driving test and that this had to be taken on a driving-school car. Robert had no difficulty with this, but I was mortified to find that I could not drive the left-hand drive car, and had to have some lessons first! The instructor was a nice elderly man who concluded I was a very nervous character and looked after me carefully, even insisting on sitting in the back of the car during the test to make sure the examiner did not rattle me – a charming attention. I knew I was suffering from a strange confusion due to left-handedness.

Through the winter Antonio, our architect, had been working on plans for our new house, and they were completed soon after our arrival. Several building firms sent in estimates – unexpectedly high ones since building costs had suddenly soared. A firm was chosen and a price agreed. We had expected that we should have to bring the money out from England to pay, with permission of the Bank of England and paying the premium on it, but Antonio suggested a mortgage. We were surprised to find out that the Savings Bank would lend us the money although we were foreigners, and Antonio explained that mortgages in Spain are based on the value of the land. So we applied for the amount of money we needed and in due course we were granted just half. Antonio laughed at our disappointment.

"I'm sorry, I forgot to tell you that they always do that. You should have asked for twice the amount you wanted. It doesn't matter. When the house is half-built and you need more money, then you can apply again. Your land with a half-built house on it will be more valuable than before, so you will get more money."

To obtain a mortgage, we had first to have the property registered at the Land Registry. There they asked for evidence from our bank of how the money had come into Spain to pay for it – a very reasonable request but which involved us in more "paper chasing" and involved Roderick too, as he had paid by proxy and so had to obtain a paper from his bank.

So, round and round we went, filling in forms, waiting more or less patiently in offices, asking for help and advice. We wondered how it was that the whole of Spain did not sink under the weight of paper collected in public offices. Once I said this aloud in our *Ayuntamiento*, and Antolín answered me that the paperwork had been simplified in recent years – there used to be more.

There is a very useful institution in Spain called a *Gestoría*. This is an office, privately run, whose staff act as go-betweens for its clients between them and officialdom. At first we supposed that a *Gestor* was a "fixer" who would find ways, maybe illegal or semi-illegal, round a client's difficulties but this was not normally so, though certainly sometimes. The *Gestoría* is an essential part of the system and there are some papers that a private person could simply not obtain at all. It would have helped us a great deal if we had found this out sooner.

"Come back tomorrow" – time has a different, an elastic, quality in Spain. "Tomorrow" may mean simply "not today". Sometimes I could bear it, sometimes I laughed, but there was at least one occasion when frustration built up to breaking point and I sat down on the front step of the house on my return from "officialdom" and wept with fatigue and fury.

In those early days we thought we would learn how to deal with all this, and it is true that many of our troubles were because we were beginners at the game. Once we had understood the *Gestoría* system and were clients of one, we could get clear and reliable help. Nevertheless there were traps for the unwary: what happened last time might be no help this time, either because the regulations had changed or simply the interpretation of them.

In 1970 we bought a new Spanish car and had a tow-bar for the trailer fitted to it. The garage then warned us that we must get the fitting inspected and passed by *Industrias* (something like the Factory Inspectorate) before we could use it, and we had to line up in a long queue of cars and lorries on a given morning and await our turn for a thorough check of the attachment and of the trailer lights.

Later, Robert was stopped by the traffic police one day when he was towing the trailer, and fined for not having a safety chain between car and trailer; they brushed aside his protest that the fitting had been passed by *Industrias* just two years previously, and said that a safety chain must be fitted within fifteen days or the fine would be much more. Easier said than done. Neither our garage nor several others knew how it had to be done. In the end someone suggested a car-body workshop and there, yes, they knew what was required.

"How could we have known it was necessary?" I asked.

"You couldn't know, *Señora*. They changed the regulations a little while ago, and I suppose they published the new ones in the Official Bulletin, but who reads that? We only know because we were fined too – for towing the breakdown crane without a safety chain." Just one of those things!

In 1977 we bought another car and before we took delivery we had a trailer bar fitted (and safety chain) and we asked the *Gestoría* to make an appointment for us in the *Industrias* inspection queue. They phoned us urgently next day to say that now, this year, we had to start by asking permission to fit a trailer bar and therefore we must present the car for inspection in the condition in which it had come from the factory. The fine for making modifications to a car without permission was 5,000 *pesetas* and recently someone had been fined for doing just that. So we must get the garage to take the bar off and the light plugs, quickly.

Apparently the matter had ended there, but fifteen years or so later, I decided to sell the trailer and discovered that I could not do so because somehow we had managed to import it without going through the proper channels and it had never been matriculated and so had always been illegally on the road!

Everyone had to waste endless time over formalities, not only because such formalities were complicated or unnecessary – though they might be – but because public relations at that time were so bad that the regulations were not set out clearly and were always being changed. A cynical friend commented – perhaps unjustly? – that the government needed a lot of money for road repairs, so when they were short they sent out the traffic police to fine motorists for offences they had never heard of. Be that as it may, the other side of the matter was equally harmful because, at that time, the Spaniards we knew would not dream of using a seat belt in their cars, or putting a safety chain on their trailers unless obliged by law, however much it were demonstrated that these were valuable safety measures.

Part Two

Getting Established

16   *Farmyard.*

17 Parish Church.

18 Village Market: "Buy my prize goats."
19 Dealing in cows.

20 Village Market. Letting out surplus milk.
21 "And now to go home".

22 Twelfth century chapel by main road.
23 Modern school opposite it.

24 *Old mortuary: new niches.*
25 *Old well and washing place: a new house.*

26 *Pontvedra Market.*

27 *The new house.*

14

The Fiesta

"A mesa mata máis xente que a guerra." (Gallego saying)
Eating kills more people than war does.

When we had bought La Saleta we had been told about the annual *fiesta*, traditionally held each Whitsunday. Doña Sofía, the owner of the property from 1911 until she died in 1964, aged ninety, was a very religious woman and for her, the Mass in the chapel was the important part of the occasion. She used to engage a group of friars from the monastery at Poyo to sing and to preach. They would come early to hear confessions – "Much more satisfactory for the people than confessing to the village priest," commented Eugenio. The Mass had great merit because it was the last chance in the religious year to fulfil one's obligations towards the church.

In bygone times, we were told, there were great jollifications after Mass, bag pipers and dancing, and the roasting of goats on the grass in front of the chapel. All this had lapsed because Doña Sofía was not interested in such matters. She used to have a lunch party in the house to which she invited the priest and the friars, while her staff, helpers and caretakers feasted in the beehive room. A very substantial lunch will have been served.

Since Doña Sofía's death there had been no celebration at all, and we were asked if we would revive the tradition. Although we were not Catholics, it seemed to us that it would be right to do so if that was what our neighbours wanted; also we thought, rightly, that it would help to integrate us into the life of the community around us. All the same, it was a strange responsibility to have taken on, and of course in 1970 we had no idea how to set about it. The date that year was to be 17th May.

One evening in the middle of March, Don Maximino, the priest, came to call on us. He was a tall thin man in a shabby cassock, often in poor health and rather shy; he always wore a beret to cover his nearly bald head, and was reluctant to take it off for fear of catching cold. We grew quite fond of him, although we came from such different worlds that points of contact were inevitably limited.

That first visit proved sticky as, very naturally, he was nervous and uncertain whether he would be able to communicate with us at all: rich, heretical foreigners speaking little Spanish.

We offered him a drink. No, the bishop had been to lunch with him that day and had only just left, and they had spent a long time *de sobremesa* (literally "over the table"), a term which means sitting and talking and drinking, still at table, after the meal is finished. Perhaps the bishop had told him to come, or perhaps his good meal with the bishop – and he would have provided an excellent and ample meal – together with plenty of wine, brandy and conversation, had given him the courage to come to see us at last.

He said he was sorry he did not speak any English, no, nor any French. He had been twenty-five years in the parish and had seen many changes. Now there was poverty but no real hunger.

We broached the subject of the *romería*, and he said it was just as we, the *señores*, wished. We said that we understood we had to ask some monks to come from the monastery.

"Oh," he said, "you don't need to bother with them. That would be expensive and unnecessary. I can ask the priests from the neighbouring parishes to come and help me say Mass."

We tried again and said that we should like to have the monks, but how did we go about asking them? Don Maximino explained that we should go and see the Father Superior – no, not write a letter. He would come with us if that would help, and so it was agreed that we would, all three, go to the monastery one day the following week. Yes, midday would be a suitable time.

Then we said that we thought of engaging some bag-pipers so as to make a real *romería*.

"Oh," he said, "that would be expensive and unnecessary. I don't like such things very much."

After a little more general conversation, Don Maximino made his escape, probably with relief. Eugenio told us later that he had always been a sad man, and when he first came to the parish he had stopped the old custom of taking the statue of the patron saint out in procession around the village. The most he would allow was that the Virgin might be taken in procession on the day of the summer village *fiesta*, from the church down the steps and around the stone cross at their foot, and back up again.

So we went to the monastery with Don Maximino, who had now more or less recovered from his fear of us and was informative and helpful. The monastery of San Juan de Poyo, originally Benedictine, was taken over in 1890 by the Mercedarios, that is the monks of the Order of Mercy. This order was founded in the thirteenth century with the purpose of rescuing Christian captives from the Moors, who were then occupying Spain. It had become a missionary and teaching order and the monastery was a training college for missionaries.

The imposing, solid grey stone building, flanked by the Baroque frontage of its church, stands on the hillside overlooking Pontevedra Bay. Just inside the front door, Don Maximino pulled the bell rope and a distant clanging could be heard; there was a long pause and then a monk came down the elegant stone staircase and showed us into a small waiting room. Another pause and the Father Superior joined us, a stout man, very courteous and benevolent – my dream of a Father Superior.

Don Maximino introduced us and explained who we were and that we wished to celebrate the traditional *romería* at La Saleta on Whitsunday. No, we were not Catholics. The Father Superior agreed to send us two fathers, one of whom would preach, and four or five students to sing. They could bring their own harmonium. Don Maximino asked quietly and discreetly about the cost, and the Father Superior answered equally quietly but promptly: about 150 pesetas each. On our way home, Don Maximino told us that he had worried about this question and was thankful to have got such a straight, clear answer as he had feared that the Father Superior would say "as the *señores* wish", which would have left us no wiser. The Mass should be at one p.m. and we should fetch the monks at about twelve. We said that we hoped they would stay to lunch afterwards, which Don Maximino had told us would be the correct thing to do.

The business of the visit now completed, the Father Superior showed us round parts of the monastery, telling us that there were about a hundred students and thirty staff. When the students, aged seventeen to twenty-four, had finished their training, they were sent all over the world, but mainly to South America. We crossed a beautiful enclosed courtyard with cloisters and camellias. The old monastery buildings were ancient and damp so they had recently built a new block of living quarters and had nearly finished a new modern chapel. This was absolutely plain except for big stained-glass windows, a huge mosaic picture each side of the altar, and two huge mosaic picture-sequences along the side walls. The mosaics had been made by a group of fourteen students working in a workshop at the back of the monastery, and had taken two years to make. Previously they had decorated a whole wall of their new dining room with a mosaic picture of the Last Supper.

Since then, years ago now, this monastery was closed because of the lack of students. The Catholic Church in Spain is seriously threatened in its work by the shortage of young men wishing to enter religious orders or to study for the priesthood. In the modern world there are so many varied opportunities for those with ideals, and celibacy is no longer acceptable to many. It is sad when a venerable institution comes to the end of its days.

Eugenio came to see us and told us that he had been making enquiries around and the neighbours wanted a dance in the evening, rather than music at midday. After Mass they would all be going home for lunch, and it was an occasion when members of their families who were living elsewhere would come to join the celebrations. By the evening they would be ready for dancing which would take place on the green in front of the chapel – if we agreed. We needed to engage a band and we would need some outside lights, and a bandstand...

"But that won't cost you anything; we'll make that with some planks."

"What about wine?"

"Someone with a bar will bring some barrels up on his cart and sell wine. That's not your problem either. But you must be sure to negotiate for the band to play for so many hours without dinner. Otherwise they will go away and eat somewhere, and take a very long time about it. Much too long! There are two rates of pay, I'm told – with dinner or without."

In reality, Eugenio was somewhat naïve about this, as we discovered in due course. Whatever the bargain made, the band would go away in the middle of the evening to have their dinner, and stay away what seemed an inordinate amount of time. Maybe it was different in the past, but dance bands became spoilt. With more money around in the countryside for such luxuries, they are able to ask for more and more pay, and insist on a good dinner as well. "Without dinner" turned out, that first year, to mean that we should pay more and that they should arrange for their own meal and pay for it. In subsequent years we found that it was only possible to engage a band "with dinner", which gave us the choice of providing the meal or of paying for it in a nearby bar. They expect soup, fish, meat courses, with wine, followed by coffee and brandy, and they have no intention of hurrying over it. The dancers must wait, or the organisers must provide bag-pipers to fill in the gap, or a second band, who, also, must have dinner. It's a long night's work though, to play and sing from about eight p.m. till two-thirty a.m., nowadays much later.

In the ordinary way, a village dance, on the annual saint's day for example, is organised by a committee of young people who go round the houses collecting the money to pay for it. In many cases the funds are boosted by large donations from villagers living or working abroad. In earlier times, emigrants who had done well used to send money back to establish a school or to build a new washing place, but now the government was providing new schools, there were fewer suitable outlets for such donations, and what could be better than helping to give the village a good *fiesta*, all the more since rivalry between villages is very keen. The more noise, fireworks, band, loudspeakers – the better.

Eugenio had found out that the gentleman who organised dance-bands was to be found in the Bar Gloria in Pontevedra, and came with us to find him. His name was *Señor* Expósito, which I took to mean "the *señor* of exhibitions" but this guess was wildly wrong. It is a real surname and means "foundling", and some forbear must have been left "exposed to the weather". *Señor* Expósito had a white, round and completely dead-pan face. He gave us a list of available bands, six or seven of them, ranging from five to ten performers, and costing from £50 up to twice that amount. We took the list home to think about it.

We asked María-Ester which of the smaller bands was good and she consulted her young friends, only to come back with the judgement that none was. So we said that perhaps it would be better to wait until another year to lay on a dance, when we would be able to start earlier and would know better how to organise it. Oh no! One of those smaller bands would be better than nothing, she said. We had no idea whether we were in danger of being taken for a ride, and Eugenio was no help because he was so horrified at the price anyway.

So we took the plunge and engaged a small group and *Señor* Expósito gave us a temporary contract with them, and a list of the permits we would need, and the steps we had to take to get them. I summarise:

★

Step one: visit to our village *Ayuntamiento* where the clerk wrote a letter, on Robert's behalf, to the Civil Governor of the province, and the *Alcalde* added a note at the bottom. I translate:

Políza: 3 pesetas   Municipal stamps: 25 and 5 pesetas.

MOST EXCELLENT SEÑOR CIVIL GOVERNER OF THE PROVINCE OF PONTEVEDRA

Robert Gimson, married, inhabitant of the parish of San Vicente in the municipality of Meis in this province EXPOUNDS to your Excellency with due respect:

That he proposes to hold a fiesta in the parish in which he lives on the 10th day of this coming June, in the open air, entertained by a musical and vocal group, and it is his desire that dancing should be authorised until TWO in the morning.

On account of this, here expounded to your Excellency, he REQUESTS that, subject to any information which you may consider appropriate, you will agree to concede the necessary AUTHORISATION for the celebration of these festivities.- This is a favour he hopes to receive from your Excellency whose life may God protect for many years to come.

Meis, Pontevedra. 7th May, 1970
(signed: R. Gimson)

STATEMENT BY THE MAYOR OF MEIS

The undersigned has the honour of stating that the applicant is of good conduct in every respect, and that there is no objection whatever on the part of this municipality to the granting of the requested permission for the fiesta. However your Excellency will decide.

Meis, Pontevedra.   7th May, 1970
(signed A. R.)

We paid 150 pesetas and for the *póliza* and municipal stamps, and were given a receipt. Time taken: three-quarters of an hour.

Step two: take the letter, the receipt and the provisional contract to the Trades Union Delegation. Pay 331 pesetas and receive a work contract for the band. The office was difficult to find and busy. Time taken: one hour at least.

Step three: take all these papers to the Civil Governor's office, pay 200 pesetas and for one *póliza* in exchange for a promise that the *permiso* would come by post in due course. Time taken: perhaps half an hour.

Step four: less urgent but still required: a paper from the representative of the local Society of Authors. It proved difficult to obtain because this gentleman had no office. He lived on a farm some ten kilometres away but was seldom at home, nor did he answer letters or respond to messages except possibly at the last moment. About two days before our *fiesta* I made a third visit to the farm at a time when I thought he would be having his lunch, which was about two-thirty when I had finished mine, and this time I found him. However, before he would attend to my request, he insisted that I sit down with his family and join in their lunch, fried fish followed by *borrachas* (drunken women) which are slices of bread soaked in wine and fried. Then there was coffee and brandy. Time taken: two hours plus two previous attempts to find him at home.

Step five: a lighting permit, but this is another story. On the four occasions we gave a *romería* dance we never once managed to get one, in spite of genuine and repeated attempts.

★

The whole exercise, like so many others, seemed just one more complicated game of snakes and ladders.

Then there was the problem of the lunch. Who should we ask and how should we do it? At that time we had no more than five dinner plates with us, and very few cooking utensils, because everything else was with our furniture waiting to start out from England. Our first idea was a buffet lunch.

"Oh no," said Eugenio, horrified. "Everyone always sits down to lunch and we can lend you some chairs. People would talk…"

I sought advice from Marina, the *Alcalde*'s wife, who had very definite ideas: certainly we must have a formal sit-down lunch with four courses at least. A starter course, fish, meat, and "afters". There should be red wine with the earlier courses and champagne with the sweet, which should be ice-cream. We had counted up and reckoned that this party would have to come to about twenty people: the monks, the *Alcalde* and Marina, the doctor and his wife, Don Maximino, and Roderick and Ana. It was obvious that I could not cook a meal on this scale with the equipment I then had, and Marina suggested that one of the bars or restaurants might do it for us. She told me that for weddings in the village the custom was to engage a woman to come and cook, and she would light a fire outside in the yard and cook everything there. She would, of course, demand a number of helpers, material for the fire and so on.

So we thought this over, and then went to ask the advice of Milucho, the owner-cook of the Casa Rosita. Usually a glum man, he was interested in the problem. No, they could not come and do the whole lunch for us as they had a wedding that day in the restaurant, but perhaps they could make some simple dishes just ready to warm up and serve, or he could recommend a woman to come and cook – that might be better – but he was not on speaking terms with her so I would have to find and talk to her myself.

"But it's still only April and much too soon to be worrying about it. Come back and see me at the beginning of May."

One evening I went to see Celina. I found the whole family out in the field in front of the house where Eugenio was trying to teach his new horse to plough. Celina said it was a terrible animal; it had taken Eugenio two hours to bring it from Pontevedra that morning, kicking and shying all along the fifteen kilometres of road. He must sell the brute again at the next possible market – a wild beast that it was!

When I could distract her attention from the dangers of the horse, I got a lot of helpful advice. María-Ester and her sister Carmen could come and help serve the lunch, and I should ask the priest to send the boy who helped with Mass, the *monaguillo* (little monk), to serve the wine, which should be freshly drawn from the barrel into bottles to put on the table. The monks should sit at a separate table.

"Why?" I asked.

"Well," said Celina, "they won't have anything to say to ordinary people, and no one will have anything to say to them."

"And they eat such a lot!" added María-Ester. "It might be embarrassing for them."

However, as they assured me that no formal seating arrangements were expected, I decided to let that matter settle itself on the day, although I only intended to provide one long table.

A second visit to the Casa Rosita settled the details of the lunch satisfactorily: I would make soup and a sweet course and they would make us a fish salad and a big pot of stewed veal with potatoes in it, which we could warm up at the last moment. When would I fetch the dishes? I said it would have to be before eleven a.m. as the Land Rover was needed to fetch the monks at twelve. Milucho said that the food could not possibly be ready before one p.m. as, of course, the salad had to be made that day. He called his son over for a consultation, and the latter said that as the wedding was not going to be very big, he could bring our dishes to the house.

Milucho told me where to hire crockery, and Lolita lent us tables and benches. Posters caused me more worry. Could we advertise the Mass and the dance on the same poster? And how would we distribute them? Lolita said that distribution was easy as she would ask the two bakers in the village to take them around in their vans to all the little shops – they went everywhere. Mass and dance on the same poster? Why not? Well, maybe the priest would not like it as he was not at all keen on dances in any case. A bystander chimed in to say that he was sure he had seen posters with both events on. Aurea, Lolita's mother, was consulted:

"Why don't you go and ask Don Maximino? Everyone likes to be consulted and if you ask him he won't like to say no."

The best time to find Don Maximino was when he came in for breakfast after celebrating early Mass. He ushered me into his study, a bare room except for a desk and two chairs. Yes, it would be all right about the posters, though there was no need for posters – he would tell the people. Yes, his boy – I noticed that he called him the *sacristán* not the *monaguillo* – would come to serve the wine; he would order him to and tell him what to do. It was a pity his elder brother was not still *sacristán*, as he did it very well and always used to help when the bishop came to lunch, but this one could learn. Yes, he would come to look what vestments and what silver and altar cloths were needed. I asked him about flowers to decorate the chapel – did it matter what flowers we used? Were there any superstitions, any kinds of flower that were taboo?

"Nothing like that!" he laughed. "It's just as you wish, *señora*."

There were plenty of other details to attend to. We fetched the chapel silver from the previous owners, who were looking after it for us, and found that it had been neglected and needed a lot of cleaning. We got the priests' vestments out of the sacks hanging up in the beehive room out of the way of the mice, and put them out in the sun to air. We consulted Ventura, the carpenter, about repairing the chapel balcony and the broken window, and he promised to come, but no, he was too busy to help build a bandstand – Eugenio and Ernesto could do that.

The last week came. It rained and nothing was nearly ready. Eugenio reminded us about lighting outside for the dance, and we walked along the track to call on the electricity boss, who was all smiles. He explained to us that really we needed a *permiso* to put up outside lights, but, never mind, it was rather too late now and he thought we need not bother. He would send Pedro along to do it at the last moment, at dusk on Sunday evening. A wire could simply be taken out of the house, a very small matter.

"You can give a tip to Pedro as he'll come out of working hours, and the current will go through your meter, but there's nothing else to pay."

Thursday afternoon. Ventura and his brother came with the new chapel window and some boards to repair the balcony, and worked right on into the dusk to finish. Eugenio and Ernesto set to work to clear away some big stones which would be in the way of dancers on the green, and María-Ester brought the horse and two cows to "mow" the grass – not quite so easy as one might think as she had to keep removing their droppings. Don Maximino came to inspect the vestments and silver. It rained.

On Friday the hired crockery was delivered and had to be checked, and the sticky pieces washed. I ironed albs and (mice-nibbled) altar cloths, and made tomato soup and chocolate mousse. It rained.

In the afternoon I went around the *finca* looking at the wild flowers we might be able to use for decorating the chapel, and here came up against a difficulty. No, foxgloves would not do, María Ester said. They were not a "serious" flower, everyone would laugh. No, yellow daisy-like flowers would not do, because yellow was not a suitable colour and everyone would talk. Flowers should be blue, white or red. Well, we had some arum lilies and some white watsonias and that was all.

So on Saturday morning I went to Pontevedra market and, advised by Celina, bought blue irises, pink watsonias, red gladioli and carnations. In the afternoon María-Ester and her sister Carmen and several of their young friends took charge of the chapel decorations, a long, untidy,

91

merry session. The altar was dressed with a gold-embroidered red frontal, covered over with the best white linen cloth with a wide lace border. Drawing pins were suddenly requested to hold it all in place. The Virgin's wig was combed out carefully and settled on her head with her brass crown on top. Then four big candleholders and two vases of the best flowers were set out on the altar. The girls climbed up and down the wobbly little stepladder to arrange small vases all around the high shelf and above the altar. The result, over-elaborate to my eyes, was much admired by everyone else. Meanwhile, I made a big arrangement of the vulgar, scorned wild flowers, yellow and mauve, for our sitting room.

Ernesto and Eugenio worked all day building the bandstand with cut pine trees and large pieces of our packing cases, and then decorated it with branches of golden broom and strings of bitter oranges hung across the top. Ventura appeared with brushes and white paint for the new window. Now we were ready.

Whitsunday dawned fine and there was sunshine all day. About midday, a steady trickle of people began to arrive for the Mass and stood around in small groups, and wandered in and out of the chapel, admiring the flowers, some of them leaving small donations on the corner of the altar. Don Maximino and his *sacristán* checked the requirements for Mass. Then the monks arrived and went to get ready; the two fathers put on lace-bordered albs and red chasubles, while the student monks connected their electric harmonium to our meter with a simple twisting of wires.

We walked around greeting our friends and acquaintances; many were difficult to recognise in their best clothes. The older women wore black, but the younger ones dressed gaily. Only a few very daring girls wore trousers. The *sacristán* tolled the bell and the crowd, perhaps two hundred strong, surged into the little chapel, leaving outside those who could not squeeze in, to listen as best they could through the open doorway. The student monks with their harmonium were up on the balcony together with so many of the men of the village that we were nervous about its safety. We never had such a crowd again as that first year; pleasure at the revival of the old custom; curiosity about us; and I believe, a genuine, warm welcome to us – all these motives must have played a part.

The singing of the monks was beautifully impressive, and the senior father preached about the co-operation between men of good will, whatever their faith, in the service of mankind. Only several years later did we discover that 1970 was the centenary of the chapel in its present form.

In some subsequent years we held the Mass outside on the green, which, provided the weather was neither too hot nor too wet, was a good solution to the question of space in the chapel and the safety of the balcony. Don Maximino said that we needed special permission from the bishop for this, but the monks brushed his objection aside, saying that there was automatic permission to celebrate Mass in the open air if there was not enough room in the chapel. This difference of opinion has its roots way back in history, because in the early days of Christianity in Galicia, some of the old religious practices of Celts and Romans became absorbed into the new cult, and therefore it was natural that the early Christian priests should have held their services on those same hill-tops and in those same oak-groves which had been used for worship from time immemorial. As the Catholic Church became more formally established and parishes were set up and churches built, attempts were made to stamp out the old open-air tradition. *Romerías*, those that are authentic, that is, date back into the distant past, continuing the tradition of a pilgrimage to a hill-top, a spring of water, or a grove of trees, believed to be sacred, often with miraculous physical or spiritual healing powers. Now, of course, the old deities have vanished, and it is the Virgin or one of the saints who presides over the spot and intercedes with God on the part of the folk who come to seek aid or blessing. Nevertheless, vestiges of pagan beliefs are still alive in country places in the form of fertility rites, fear of the evil eye, and faith in a wide range of methods of protecting oneself and one's animals from the powers of darkness. We never managed to find out whether the La Saleta *romería* dates back any further than a hundred and thirty years, from the time when Doña Sofía's father built, or maybe rebuilt, the chapel. It could possibly be significant that the hamlet in which La Saleta is situated is called *Sobreira*, which means "place of cork oak trees".

The lunch party went splendidly. We sat down sixteen to table at about two p.m., normal Spanish lunch-time. At first the monks wanted to sit all together and so did some of the ladies, but we managed to persuade them to mix up. The two fathers were highly educated, quite men of the world, but, to begin with, the students were very shy. However, once lunch was well under way, they turned into ordinary, cheerful young men, and the youngest of the party, who was sitting beside me, became quite confidential and told me details about life in the monastery in a very quiet voice. Afterwards María-Ester commented:

"What a pity nice young men like that have to be monks and wear skirts!"

Much of the conversation went too fast for us and it grew very animated. The highlight was a lively discussion about medical care in Spain, France and England, which culminated in an argument as to whether a sick person was cured by medical treatment or by faith in his doctor. The senior father maintained that it was medical skill whereas the doctor said no, it was faith.

María-Ester and Carmen and the *sacristán* ran to and fro serving the four courses, managing excellently although none of them had ever done the job before. The boy, aged thirteen and very small, served the wine solemnly, carrying a white "napkin" over his arm in imitation of a real waiter; unfortunately it was a very dirty striped tea-towel.

The party got very merry, all the more so, because we had all been nervous to start with. At the end I produced the remains of our Christmas cake, which we had brought with us three months before, and it caused much surprise. By the time lunch was over and we were showing our visitors round the *finca*, the student monks had become even noisy, and wanted to know all about us, why we had come, and when, and what for – like any villager. As they all piled into the Land Rover to go back to their monastery, Robert handed the senior father an envelope with the money in payment – "for the monastery" – and he accepted it almost reluctantly because, he said, they had had such a happy day.

Now, towards evening, the band arrived. At once they said the bandstand was too small and Ernesto and Eugenio had to set to and make it bigger. Pedro appeared and rigged up lighting. The band retired into the beehive room to change into evening dress, and at eight o'clock the music struck up as the first few people were assembling.

After a while we went out to look and were utterly astonished at the scene. There were perhaps five hundred people crowded on the green, and cars parked along the track in both directions as far as the road. About half of the people were dancing in a semi-solid mass in the middle of the area, and, all around, standing or sitting on the stone benches, were onlookers of every age and description: wrinkled old grandparents, buxom mothers, impassive-looking men, stiff in their best suits, babies in arms and children of all ages running and dancing on the fringes of the crowd.

Most of the dancing was of the cuddle and shuffle kind as the country people had no reason to learn modern dancing and had forgotten or maybe scorned the old folk dances. Already in a novel about Galicia, published in 1927, the author lamented that the young people of his village only danced tightly clutched together. Since 1970, the date of our first *fiesta*, there has been a movement, encouraged by the government, to revive folk music and dancing, and on special occasions there are fine performances by trained groups, and growing interest in the schools.

A line of bare electric light bulbs hung from a wire strung from the porch, via the bandstand across the track to an improvised bar, which was doing a huge trade. Alongside it was a stall selling sweets and the rather dry, sugar-coated cakes in the form of a ring, which seem to be an essential accompaniment of any *fiesta*.

The din the band made was unbelievable, echoing right across the valley. Conversations were shouted, children squealed and from time to time volleys of banging rockets went off. There had been bangs off and on all day, to advertise the event to the whole district, and the dance ended well after two in the morning with an enormous salvo. We had said no to rockets, but it made no difference.

"You must have fireworks at a *fiesta*. People would talk…"

We went to bed exhausted and dizzy with success. Next morning we found that the improvised lighting system had burnt out the automatic switch of the water pump.

15

Getting to know the neighbours

"Falando enténdense as xentes." (Gallego saying)
By talking, people understand each other.

The celebration of the *romería* that first year marked a definite step forward in our relationship with our neighbours and henceforward we found ourselves accepted as part of the local community, accepted, that is, as fully as is possible between people of such different levels of wealth, culture and background. Wealth is, of course, a relative term. The living standards of the village were rising fast but, inevitably, in their eyes, we seemed rich.

We celebrated the *romería* each Whitsunday with Mass in the chapel, but there was never again the same huge attendance, nor did we have quite the same thrill from the occasion. We became more efficient; the arrangements for Mass went more smoothly; I made a new altar cloth to replace the mouse-eaten one we inherited, with instructions from Lolita; the Virgin was equipped with a new wig; the lunch was more ambitious and better served, and we began to be able to hold coherent conversations in Spanish. In 1974 the monastery at Poyo was closed so we had to find other ways of providing the singing and preaching which were essential to differentiate a *fiesta* from the regular spoken Mass of every Sunday in the parish church.

We were now widely recognised around the district and aroused much curiosity. Such tall thin people! Stories about us, true or untrue, circulated. It was said that we must be cultivating drugs. Why else would anyone plant all those bushes? People engaged us in conversation at the slightest pretext. "What?" "Why?"

We began to recognise our neighbours and tried to learn their names, which was not so easy. The number of surnames in use in the district was very small. The population had been settled for many centuries, and until recently, it was not expected that young people would marry outside their own parishes, resulting in some inbreeding. A Spaniard has two surnames: first his father's and second that of his mother. In the village, one farmer might be called Benito Casal Abal, and his neighbour on one side, Juan Abal Casal, and on the other, Manuel Casal Sabarís. The women keep their own names on marriage so their two names may similarly repeat and interchange the same half dozen surnames.

Add to this confusing situation the fact that there was not a wide range of Christian names in use either, partly because it was customary to name the first girl child after her mother, and the first boy child after his father.

It was not surprising therefore that nicknames were widespread and in some cases seemed to be a kind of alternative surname whose origin went back into the past, parallel to the established surname required and recognised by the State. Two old sisters living in different houses were known as Peregrina and Dolores *de la Pesquera* (of the weir, or possibly the fishpond) which must have defined the family they came from, though there was neither weir nor fishpond anywhere near where they lived. Our friend Eugenio Mouriño Prado was known as Eugenio *del Pozo* (of the well) and his daughter, Carmen, married and living some five kilometres away, was distinguished from all the other Carmens living around her by this same *del Pozo*. I met a woman who told me that she was known to everyone as *La Cacharola* (the cooking pot), because when she and her husband had built a shop on a piece of her land, it was beside a favourite camping place of the gypsies and littered with their abandoned broken cooking pots. It seemed that it was only the demands of the State which caused surnames to be fixed at all, and that village society preferred the semi-spontaneous sobriquet.

I met Consuelo, a small round elderly woman, on a footpath one afternoon, carrying a letter in her hand. She walked very slowly, stopped every now and then to squint at the envelope and hold it up to the light. I greeted her and remarked that I hoped she had good news, and she poured out her story.

The letter was from her husband who had gone away to the Argentine forty years previously, and she had not seen him since. When he left, she had refused to go with him because she could not bear to leave her family and her home, and so she had stayed behind with their two small children and the farm. Later, when she had brought herself to the point of deciding to join him, her old parents fell ill and she had to stay to look after them. The years passed, the children grew up and married, and now there were grandchildren – surely I knew them?

Meanwhile, in the Argentine, her husband prospered. He set up and ran a small bus company, but now he was ready to retire and wanted to return to Galicia. But suddenly, Argentine money was worth so little that perhaps he would not be able to come.

"I have heard that there was great poverty here forty years ago," I said. "Was there real hunger?"

"Yes," she said. "There was great distress and hunger. We always had enough to eat because we owned land and because we had only two children. Now it is different. Even the poorest can live, because a day wage brings in enough to eat."

Some months later I noticed a distinguished-looking white-haired stranger along our track, and when I asked who he was, I was told that he was Consuelo's husband, who had indeed returned. Then I met them together, and she flung her arms round me and introduced me to him with tears in her eyes. However, the story ended in tragedy. He developed cancer the following year, and, within fifteen months of his return, he was dead.

In the past it was not unusual that the wife should be left alone at home, struggling to keep the farm going and to bring up the children. For centuries there was emigration from Galicia; the region is mountainous and rocky, and the farms are tiny. There was a long history of oppression, by nobles in feudal times, then by the Church, which was the largest landowner when the unruly nobles had been suppressed, and in modern times by the centralised government in Madrid, who, until recently, took little interest in this poor and backward corner of

Spain. Farming traditions and methods remained largely medieval and it was only in the years since the Civil War that the modern world began making an impact.

In earlier centuries, many Galicians emigrated to the richer parts of Spain and to Portugal, often to work as servants; seasonal workers went off to help with the harvest in Castile; and from time immemorial they were sailors and fishermen. Then, with the colonisation of South America, great opportunities opened up for enterprising young men, and the Galicians took full advantage of these, many making successful new lives. But great suffering was caused to families at home, and the effects on the region of this continual loss of the some of the ablest of the men were certainly damaging. Some successful emigrants returned, either to visit their families, or to settle down at home again in their old age, and money was often sent back, but many families were permanently broken up. Some married men forgot their wives left at home and settled down with other women and raised second families, whilst their wives, *viudas de vivos* (widows of the living), waited and waited for news which perhaps never came.

Since the Second World War the pattern of emigration has changed, and, from the point of view of family life and of the village community, things have improved. Now the restless and ambitious young men go to work in the industrialised countries of Western Europe, which means that they come back for holidays. The wives can accompany their men and both can earn good money. But many have little aptitude for foreign languages and have poor basic education, so they arrive in the host country utterly unprepared, live and work closely huddled together and suffer severely from home sickness, all of which means that they are often unable to profit fully from their opportunities. Nevertheless, they may return with substantial savings, available to rebuild homes, perhaps set up a bar or a shop or buy a tractor, and the quality of their lives will have been improved.

The reason for so much emigration was that the ordinary small farm could not support more than one adult married member, with spouse and children. The others had to seek other work, and in the region, until recently, there was almost no industry and few sizeable towns. The typical traditional farm household consisted of three generations living under one roof, and the old grandparents kept control of the money coming in, and of the land and its use until their death, when the land and resources would be divided between their children.

The Galician inheritance system is rather complicated. The parent can leave one fifth of his estate as he chooses, and one third, called *la mejora* (the betterment) to whichever of his children has stayed at home and helped with the farm, often an unmarried daughter or youngest child. The remainder of the estate must be divided equally among his children, including the one who has already had this special benefit. The system dates at least from the sixteenth century and is maybe of Visigoth origin. It results in people owning minute pieces of land, often distant from where they live, and the farms get smaller and smaller. Celina owned a piece of woodland across the valley and a tiny maize field some five kilometres in the other direction. She would not consider selling the small field because it had belonged to her grandmother.

In order to improve agricultural efficiency, the government started a scheme to re-allocate the land in the villages so that each family should have a group of fields close together, a slow and difficult business, since the farmers of each parish had to agree to the plan, and then agree to what was proposed.

Where family relationships are good, these multi-generational households are happy and well balanced. The old people are well looked after and generally usefully involved in the daily life of the farm. They take out the cows or one or two sheep or goats, and they bring in loads of grass or firewood. The last summer of her life, Ernesto's grandmother insisted upon taking on the responsibility for stripping the maize grains from the cobs, and day after day she went to the *alpendre* and worked at her task until it was finished.

Bad family relationships are terrible. Rosa and Emilio and their young daughter lived in the farm next to us. Rosa's old mother, who lived with them, was difficult and bad-tempered and at times off her head. (Eugenio told me that she was unmarried, but had been so easy to lay that it was surprising that she had only one child.) Emilio had married Rosa with the expectation that they would inherit the farm, but he must have paid dearly for it since they all quarrelled incessantly and passionately. There were occasions when Rosa threw buckets of cold water over the old woman, who was finally admitted to the *asilo* (old people's home), but not before Rosa and Emilio had got her, during a fit of insanity, to make over the farm to them. They were strongly criticised by their neighbours for this, and even ostracised for a time. However, the *asilo* then demanded a quarter of the crops from the farm to pay for the old mother's keep, so they fetched her home again. But fortunately now medical science came to their aid, and the old woman was put on a tranquillising drug, and the last two years of her life were peaceful and bearable for her family.

Not only was life harsh for many of these families, but also there was a lot of violence. Quarrels about water rights, the exact boundary of a field, a wrongly cut-down tree, or damage to young trees by a cart, these and many other matters gave rise to fierce disputes, and could end in tragedy.

Two families in our lane lived side by side, sharing the entrance and yard. On one side of the yard lived Modesto and his wife, a quiet elderly couple. Modesto had the reputation for being grumpy at times, but was well liked. On the other side lived *El Rato* (the rat) and his wife, inevitably known as *La Rata*. He once told me that his nickname had been given to him in childhood and that people sometimes addressed him as *Serafín Rato* as if it were his real surname. *La Rata* was a talkative woman, something of a busybody, but better liked on the whole than her husband.

One day the two wives quarrelled, and were still at it when Modesto came in from the fields carrying his mattock over his shoulder. Suddenly he lost his temper and hit *La Rata* over the head with his mattock. He was arrested and she died in hospital a week later from brain injury. In due course Modesto was sentenced to seven years in jail for homicide, and it would have been a much longer sentence had not several of his neighbours gone to court to speak on his behalf.

Fortunately for Modesto's wife, the house they lived in and the farm still belonged to his old mother, so could not be seized to pay compensation to *El Rato* and the two families continued to live side by side. *El Rato* rebuilt part of his house to face in the other direction and he built a wall across the middle of the shared yard. When Modesto came out of prison, he and his wife went to live with their married daughter in a new house down the lane and their poor little house was left standing empty and abandoned.

16

The village

"Un medico cura, dous dudan, e tres…morte segura." (Gallego saying)
One doctor cures, two are doubtful, and three…certain death.

In the autumn of 1970 building work started on our new house, and from then until the spring of 1972 we watched the new house grow, while continuing to live in the old house. Considerable supervision of the work was necessary because an architect in Galicia did not expect to supervise the details of building work. He drew up the plans, negotiated a price with a building firm and engaged an *aparejador*. This latter was paid separately and directly by the client; he should act as go-between between client, builder and architect, and check the quality and quantity of materials used, to make sure the client was not cheated. Ours was not very useful, rarely appearing and not really competent. The whole main floor of the building turned out to be eight centimetres too low when the work was almost finished. Our architect, by now a personal friend, made more visits to inspect progress, and to disentangle our difficulties, than he would normally have expected to do, but the day-to-day supervision, checking of details, builders' queries et cetera fell on Robert's shoulders, and there were endless difficulties because of his inadequate Spanish and our different cultural backgrounds.

There were many vicissitudes. We had periods of elation when we rejoiced in good progress, and periods of depression when the strangest things went wrong, not only common delays such as the non-delivery of materials, but the omission of a whole doorway when a fly had sat down on the builders' plan. On one occasion we were surprised to see the crane being taken away, and when we asked why, we were told that it was required for five days in order to make a concrete saluting base for a "spontaneous" demonstration in honour of a visit by General Franco! Finally we settled into our new house in March 1972, after moving in and out again once, because the wooden floors came up in a ridge, across the middle of the main room.

It seemed luxurious indeed. The old house was delightful in summer, but cold and damp in winter. Now we had central heating and could expect our clothes and bedding to be dry all winter; we had space to spread out and could work at different activities without getting in each other's way. I now had a fine modern kitchen with the aids I had been used to in England, and we could get the washing machine working again – no more washing clothes, sheets and all in the bath. All this and the wonderful views from every window! The garden was beginning to take shape too, and once the builders' mess had been cleared away, Robert could start to plant up the near terraces, and make paths and flower beds around the house

By now our Spanish had improved considerably and we had gradually pieced together a general idea of the mechanism of local affairs. The area of local administration was the municipality, administered by the *Ayuntamiento* (council) Our municipality was about twenty square miles. The *alcalde* presided over the *Ayuntamiento*, advised by eight councillors, who were elected by the villagers, and met every three months, and assisted by two deputies whom he chose himself from among the councillors. Until 1976 the *alcalde* was appointed by the Civil Governor and therefore had to be a sound Franco supporter. Since 1976 *alcaldes* were elected by the villagers. The job was not popular: unpaid except for small expenses, it took a lot of time, although certainly there were perks, and it gave its holder a good deal of local power and influence, as well as status. Lolita's husband, Don Jorge, was *alcalde* during most of our time, and a good, if solidly conservative one, and very expert at settling personal disputes.

The day-to-day work of the *Ayuntamiento* was done by the secretary, a qualified lawyer, assisted by several clerks, typists and messengers.

They collected car and cart taxes, a tax on new buildings, and the annual tax on land and houses – the equivalent of our rates. The *Ayuntamiento* would have been responsible for local sanitation, rubbish disposal, street lighting and water supplies, if these had existed.

At that time, there were a few street lights in our village centre, and a small water scheme that supplied piped water from a spring in the mountainside to some of the houses around the market place. As far as I know there were no sewage arrangements; each house owning a bathroom and WC must have put in their own septic tank. Those with no bathroom used the stable. There were no provisions for rubbish disposal whatsoever, and piles of rubbish were just dumped by the roadside, in woodlands and even in the corners of farmyards. In the old days, there would have been practically no rubbish in the countryside: left-over food went to the animals, clothing was worn to the bitter end and then used as rags, and rags rot eventually and so do old shoes, though their soles may be useful for making home-made tap washers so it was wise to keep a few suitable pieces of sole in a crack in your wall for use in emergencies. Bottles were re-used, since every farm family made their own wine and not much paper can have been used since the majority of country people were at best semi-literate.

However as living standards rose, the juxtaposition of a traditional rural way of living with the arrival of modern aids-to-living produced a flood of tins, bottles, old bits of farm machinery, and, worst of all, plastic in all its forms, which had to be disposed of somehow. The average countryman was slow to see what a mess the rubbish was making of his beautiful countryside but gradually things improved, and ultimately the rubbish began to be collected from roadside bins, which were often overflowing.

The population of Galicia lives widely dispersed in hamlets of anything from four to twelve houses, rather than in compact villages as in Castile. Each parish has perhaps ten or twelve such hamlets and the church often stands alone higher up the hillside, presiding over the homes of the parishioners in the valley below. The municipality will include a number of parishes.

The present system of municipalities in Spain dates from 1836 and since then, for practical reasons, larger groups of houses tend to have grown up around the *Ayuntamiento*: that is where the market place is, the doctor's house, maybe a chemist's shop, the post office, and a number of small shops and bars.

When we arrived in the village, and for the next fifteen years, the doctor, Don José, lived with his wife and eight children in a small house near the *Ayuntamiento*. He was very intelligent and hard-working with a high reputation for miles around. He had a small salary from the state and had a list, provided by the *Ayuntamiento*, of poor people to be treated free. Workers were covered by compulsory state insurance. The majority of the villagers, self-employed farmers, paid the doctor, often partly in kind, unless they were members of a private insurance scheme run by one of them. Don José consistently refused to accept payment from us, as his friends, but fortunately his children needed coaching in English and from time to time we could give him a bottle of whisky, and occasionally we could bring him a banned book, published in South America, from England. He had served with Franco's army during the Civil War, but was increasingly interested to read other opinions. He used to half-ask me how it was that we had had only three children whereas he had eight – "Thanks to God, all healthy."

He held surgery in his house every morning and as there was only a tiny waiting room, most of his patients waited outside by the roadside. However if they were "friends", they were ushered into the family living room and got priority attention. In the afternoon he did visits. He told us that when he started to practise in the village after the end of the Civil War, there had been so few roads that he visited his patients on horseback, and then later on a motorbike.

Not only was he famous for the quality of his care, but also for his hot temper and the noisy quarrels which erupted from time to time between him and his wife, audible from the road outside the house.

Since he retired in the 1980s, the village has a new young doctor and everything has become more formal, with a health centre in the enlarged house, and now there is a health service for all.

Even in the 1970s, isolated country and mountainous districts must have been very poorly served because of footpaths and cart tracks between hamlets or farms, poor or non-existent telephone service, wild rainy weather in the winter with snow in the mountains. So naturally there was a long tradition of witches, black or white, healers and wise women, with their semi-magical practices and range of herbs and potions. Even in our village I was told that many families still consulted the wise woman rather than the doctor, or as well as the doctor – just in case. No one would tell me who she was. The Galicians say, "We don't believe in witches, but yes there are some."

In the winter of 1970, we ourselves were involved in an unorthodox medical matter that caused us considerable anxiety. Celina had some long-standing trouble with her back. The pain came and went, but at times prevented her from working and caused her much misery. She told me she thought the damage had been done at the birth of her youngest child when the neighbour who was helping "pulled too hard". Now she and Eugenio had heard that there was a "*señor*" – not a doctor – who was very clever with bones and who had cured other people with similar trouble, and they were wondering whether to consult him.

One evening in November, Eugenio came to tell us that they had been to consult this man, and that he was to come the following Thursday afternoon to treat Celina's back. Would we be so kind as to fetch him in our car and take him back home afterwards? They had thought about a taxi, but the treatment would take some time and the taxi would have to wait, and then would be very expensive. We were not at all pleased at the idea of getting involved in such a matter, but it would have been churlish to refuse, especially considering how much time and trouble Eugenio and Celina had given to our problems.

Eugenio explained that the man was a bone-setter who dealt equally with people and animals. He would manipulate Celina's back and then strap it up with sticking plaster for twelve days, during which time she must stay in bed. Naturally Celina was very frightened as she had heard that the treatment was painful.

We agreed that I should go with Eugenio to fetch the bone-setter and that Robert would take him back afterwards, so Eugenio and I set off about three p.m. The man lived in a village the far side of Pontevedra and had promised to be ready at three-thirty, but, when we reached the house there was no one there except his apparently drunken wife, who had only the vaguest idea where he might be. We waited and waited. Then he returned, an elderly and very wheezy countryman with old, well-worn clothing and a kind, homely face, smelling strongly of garlic and farmyards. He said he had received a message that a child with a dislocated shoulder was waiting for him so he disappeared inside his house. Eugenio and I waited.

While we waited Eugenio told me that this man was very much sought after. There was another bone-setter near Vigo, but he drank too much; he was all right in the mornings, it seemed, and he held "surgery" in the mornings, but, by the afternoons, when he went visiting, he had had too much wine with his lunch. I asked whether doctors did not cope with dislocations?

"Well," said Eugenio, "doctors are good at treating broken bones but no good at dislocations. This man has some sort of permit to allow him to work, but he is not allowed to treat broken bones. They tell me that he got a permit because he cured the wife of one of the bone specialists after the doctors had not been able to do anything for her."

I asked about Celina. Had they tried the doctors?

"Yes," said Eugenio. "We went to a specialist a few years ago, but he said that the only cure would be an operation but that she was rather old for that, so she'd better have a support corset and take pills when the pain was bad. Now this chap says her back needs putting right quickly or she'll be crippled for life. She's got a bone in her spine out of place." He pointed to his side, just above his hip bone to demonstrate where the bone from her spine had got to – obviously anatomically impossible!

At last the bone setter came back. "It was a good thing they found me," he said, "the child had a broken collarbone so I set it for him." So much for the rules!

By this time it was five p.m. and I asked how long Celina's treatment would take.

"Oh, not two hours," he said. But it was all of three hours before he was ready to be taken home that evening. Eugenio said that the manipulation had been dreadfully painful and that Celina had screamed a lot.

I did not go to see Celina next day, but on Saturday I went up to the farm where I found her in a very poor state, in great pain, and she had not been able to sleep. She felt sick, she told me, and could not eat anything. Certainly she looked very ill, possibly feverish, and she lay moaning and sighing and saying she was going to die. I was horrified. Suppose she were really very ill? It was certainly my responsibility to call the doctor if so. What would Don José say, and how could I possibly explain, let alone justify, our part in this?

I fetched some aspirins and some sleeping tablets I had in the house, and gave them to her with strict instructions as to how many to take and when, and went home seriously worried.

Next morning I was exceedingly relieved to find her very much better, a different woman. The aspirins had relieved the pain and she had had a good night's sleep. Her fear had lifted and she was glad to talk, telling me about her childhood and family.

The following days must have seemed interminable to her. The strapping became very uncomfortable and the skin underneath peeled off. She could not read because she had no glasses, but it is possible that she could hardly read in any case. I was told that many of the older people who did, in fact, learn to read once, had since forgotten as they had not used the skill since their schooldays. At last the day came to start to get up a little, and I took her and Eugenio over to the bone-setter's house. He pronounced himself satisfied with the manipulation and put on some new sticking plaster, advising her how to look after her skin where the strapping had damaged it, and about how to recover her strength again. Her back was cured.

17

The pine wood

"Desconfía e acertarás." (Gallego saying)
Be suspicious and you will be right.

The new house was built with a big water tank underneath, from which the water was pumped up into the living quarters, and also across to the old house cistern. I have explained how the water came down from the spring in the pinewood behind the house in a *mina*. Now the builders installed a pipe into the channel, and built an inspection tank alongside the road. In later years, from time to time, the pipe blocked with tree roots and had to be cleared.

The wood belonged to an old lady who had several sons and one daughter, and when she died they decided they had a unique opportunity to sell it to us, for a good price, of course.

So one summer afternoon, one of the sons, Enrique, called on us. Would we like to buy the wood? Their price was 350,000 pesetas – about £600 in those days. Robert said that was too much, the subject was dropped, and we talked about the weather and the beautiful view. No doubt Enrique looked around and concluded that we were rich.

Naturally Robert went to consult Eugenio. He had acted as caretaker for this family who lived some way away.

"You'll buy it of course," said Eugenio. "It's like this. There are good people and bad people everywhere in this world and this village is like everywhere else. Suppose someone bought the wood who didn't like you. Then maybe they wouldn't let you work up there to clean out the *mina* or repair the well-head, or they could throw down a dead dog. Suppose…"

Eugenio agreed that the price was too high, but said that surely it was an opening bid. Together he and Robert examined the wood carefully. There were some good pines, ready to cut, but too many small ones that needed thinning out.

The interchange of opening bids was repeated summer after summer. The price 350,000, then 400,000. Each time Robert answered that it was too much and then wrote and offered 300,000. Each time there was no answer.

Then Eugenio came up with an interesting consideration.

"You've got neighbours' rights to the wood."

"What are those?"

"Well," he explained, "if a small piece of land is for sale, it must be offered first to the owner of the adjoining land. And even if he does not buy it then, he has the right, for a whole year, to buy it for the price a new owner has paid."

Two years passed and we heard that Enrique was busy courting. Then he turned up one evening and said that he had got another buyer, a young man who worked in Belgium and wanted to put his saved money into woodland before the end of his holiday in the village. He had offered 425,000 pesetas, Enrique said, and they were hoping to push him up to 500,000.

Robert asked if the young man knew we had the water rights.

"Yes, of course," he said. Robert repeated that the price was too high.

Two evenings later Enrique came again, this time to confirm that we were not interested, and hurried off without further conversation. As it happened, this was the night of a dance in the village, and Eugenio had no difficulty in discovering who this young man was – one Antonio, whose family we knew. Now Antonio told Eugenio that the deal had fallen through because there had been no mention of water rights, and when he had asked and suggested he should come to talk to us before agreeing to buy at 400,000 – never the 425,000 that Enrique had asked – the latter had lost his temper, shouted, "No, no, the matter must be settled now!" and rushed off, very angry.

Next day, Antonio came to see us and said that the wood was not worth as much to him without the water, and that it was clear that Enrique had tried to trick him. Evidently Enrique had tried to trick us too.

Robert wrote and offered 360,000. There was no answer. Some months later two of the other brothers visited the village accompanied by their wives. They called on Eugenio and told him they had definitely decided to sell the wood and would accept 450,000 pesetas from him or from anyone in the village, but that they would not sell it to us for less than 500,000. Then they went to the shop and wrote out a notice saying just that. This information reached us within the hour!

Baffled, Robert consulted a friend, one who knew a good deal about buying and selling of land. His friend told him that this kind of difficulty often arose. The sellers assumed that he certainly did want to buy the wood, and, after all, an outside buyer might make real trouble for him, and so they were trying to squeeze an exorbitant price out of him. His advice was to buy through a middleman, perhaps a woodcutter might be suitable. He knew of a case where a transaction of the sort had been successfully carried through. About neighbours' rights, however, Eugenio had been mistaken: because there was a track between the wood and our property, we had no neighbours' rights. Enrique never knew this.

Yet again we went to consult Eugenio, and sat in his kitchen with his wife and daughter over several glasses of wine. Everyone had their say, agreeing that Enrique's behaviour was *malo* (bad) and that this was not the correct way to conduct a negotiation. (Though Galician negotiations are not normally straightforward, but generally somewhat tortuous.)

Now Robert made his suggestion:

"Eugenio, do you know a really trustworthy woodman who would buy the wood on my behalf? Act as go-between for me?" There was a shocked silence.

Eugenio thoroughly enjoyed intrigues, but this idea alarmed him considerably. He had never thought of anything so reckless. Suppose Robert fell down dead and the woodman was left with no money to pay? Suppose the woodman fell down dead before he had handed over the wood, and his heirs refused to hand over? Suppose...and suppose... . The

1 *Aerial view of the property.*

2 Old buildings from the wood above.

3 *From terrace below, entrance to old house.*

4 Dovecote.

5 *Old house yard.*

6   *Restored old house from garden side.*

7   *Children folk-dancing after Fiesta Mass.*

8 Alterpiece in the Chapel.

discussion went round and round, Robert explaining that there would have to be a signed agreement between him and the woodman, they would have to work out the details very carefully, and it could only go wrong if the woodman was untrustworthy. Eventually Eugenio promised to think about it.

The following Sunday Eugenio brought his woodman friend, Evaristo, to our house, and the conspiracy was hatched. First it was necessary to start right at the beginning, to explain to Evaristo why direct negotiations had failed. Would he buy the wood, with our money, and sell it to us immediately afterwards? Evaristo thought this was a highly risky undertaking. Suppose Robert tricked him in some way, or went away, or fell down dead in the middle of the negotiations? He was a thoughtful, slow-moving chap, rather more educated than Eugenio perhaps, but less of a talker, and he found it impossible, at first, to understand what Robert said. Eugenio had to repeat everything in *Gallego* before he grasped it, but little by little he began to relax, and when the whole question had been reviewed at least three times – and the wine glasses filled up that number of times too – he smiled and "yes", he would do it, but only if the plan was very carefully worked out.

Once he had made the decision, the same delight in a good intrigue, as Eugenio was feeling, came over him and he settled back in his chair and leaned forward with his elbows on his knees, to plan.

To begin with, he said, he did not think that Robert had really understood that there was now a demand, a rising demand, for land at almost any price. Ridiculous prices were being paid because the country people were frightened of inflation, and as they did not trust banks they wanted to put their savings into land, especially woodland, which was a type of investment. Eugenio nodded in agreement; he had even considered buying the piece of woodland in question himself for just this reason. Evaristo then said that he thought we should be lucky if we got it for as little as 400,000 this year. He proposed that he should get in touch with this family and start to bargain, in order to find out just what price they would accept, and, when this was known, then a careful agreement about how to proceed could be worked out.

One problem was causing both countrymen a lot of worry. Suppose one of the brothers had raised a mortgage on the wood and no one else knew, and then, when the sale had gone through, the mortgagee turned up saying the wood was his? They both knew of dreadful cases of such happenings and recounted them at length. Robert reassured them by saying that the sale would be conducted through a lawyer, which should be a reasonable protection against such sharp practice. This was a new idea to the two countrymen, whose dealings in land, cattle or wine had always been conducted privately and sealed with a handshake and a glass of wine.

So, a day or so later, Eugenio and Evaristo went to visit the sellers, and Eugenio introduced his friend. Only the sister, María, was at home and she insisted the price was 500,000, but she would talk to her brothers about it. Nothing happened for a while, except that another possible buyer came to look, and, as caretaker, Eugenio showed him round. Being a great talker, he said plenty about water rights, and about the English neighbour who might, one day, want to dig up part of the wood to clean out the spring. Such talk was discouraging.

In due course, Evaristo received a letter saying that the family had agreed to accept 450,000 so he and Eugenio came to see us the following Sunday to consider what to do next.

Evaristo said, in his meditative way, that it was his opinion that it was María who was standing out for the higher price. Suppose he offered her a little something on the side, to persuade her brothers to accept 400,000? This time it was our turn to be startled and shocked!

Evaristo went on to explain that he had plenty of experience of buying woodland from large families who could not, or would not agree. Once, he said, he had to give a little bribe to every single one of the people concerned, so that each one thought he was doing better than the others!

So Evaristo went to their home again, found María alone, and after a quarter of an hour of friendly conversation, he offered her 20,000 pesetas to persuade her brothers to sell at 400,000, to be paid to her when the sale had gone through. Her eyes lit up and she agreed. A week later Enrique wrote to Evaristo agreeing that they would sell at 400,000.

By this time, Eugenio and Evaristo were thoroughly enjoying themselves; they had not had such fun for years. But events took an unlucky turn. It was arranged that Evaristo should meet the family the following Saturday morning in the lawyer's office to complete the purchase, but he fell ill with pneumonia and the appointment had to be cancelled indefinitely because some of the family would be away for Christmas.

Christmas came and went, Evaristo recovered from his illness, and in due course he phoned for an appointment. Alas! No appointment was now obtainable. María had had a stroke and lay speechless and paralysed in hospital. It seemed like the end of the affair. The wood belonged to all the brothers and María jointly, and had she died, her heirs would have had to agree to sell their share, and she had an under-age daughter and a mentally deficient son. Her husband would have had to act on their behalf – but did he know anything about the 20,000 pesetas? Meanwhile land prices continued to rise.

Six months passed without any news. Then one afternoon, two of the brothers, Jorge and Pedro, accompanied by María's daughter, came to Eugenio's house.

Eugenio gave us a graphic account of what happened. First he asked after María.

Jorge replied that she was a lot better, walking again and going out a little. Would he ask his friend to fix a date to settle the matter of the wood? And Pedro added: "The price is 450,000 pesetas."

"Oh no, Don Pedro, I beg your pardon, 400,000 pesetas," said Eugenio. Jorge then answered that prices had gone up since the previous year and now they were selling at 450,000.

Eugenio went into his house and fetched the letters. "Look, Don Jorge: here it is in writing. The deal would have gone through last winter if *Señor Dios* had not held up the sale. My friend Evaristo has agreed to pay 400,000 and no more."

Very annoyed, the two brothers left to go and talk over the matter at home. But María's young daughter held back a moment and said softly to Eugenio, "*Señor* Eugenio, Mother says please will you remind the *señor* woodman about the conversation he had with her."

Two days later Evaristo received a letter that said that, as it had been a matter of fate that the deal had not been completed earlier, they would sell at 400,000.

Now this drama seemed to be moving towards a denouement at last. Robert and I went to see the lawyer to explain, so that the deals, both of them, could go through smoothly. Then Eugenio and Evaristo made a date with the sellers. Robert got the money from the bank, in cash as was usual for property sales, and checked it very carefully.

Eugenio and Evaristo came to collect the money early on the appointed day. They both looked very smart in black suits and white shirts. A final conference took place and Robert explained that the lawyer had told us that both deals could be completed on the same day.

Ah," said Evaristo, "then we can kill two pigs with one knife!"

"Unless there is something wrong with the documents," warned Eugenio.

"Then there is no deal at all!" said Evaristo emphatically.

Robert assured them that the lawyer had promised to examine the papers very carefully. We would follow them to the town, and wait in a bar where they could find us when the first deal was completed. He handed over the money – 400,000 pesetas in a big envelope and 20,000 in a small one for María. Yes, he had counted the money very carefully. He and Evaristo signed duplicate copies of the final agreement between them, which included a receipt for the money and the two friends set off.

We waited and waited in the bar. What could have happened? When at last they arrived they were jubilant. Yes, there had been a delay. The sellers had not paid all the tax due on the wood, and Enrique had had to go and do so before the proceedings could start. As usual, Eugenio had great pleasure in telling us exactly what had taken place.

They had all crowded into the lawyer's office, he read the contract aloud, the money was counted out by his secretary and handed over, and they all signed the deed in turn.

Then Jorge asked the lawyer whether they could use a room to divide out the money and the clerk ushered them into a small room across the passage. Eugenio and Evaristo held back in the passage, and as María passed, Evaristo handed her the little envelope and she swiftly put it in her pocket. The family sat down round the table and Jorge, as the eldest, dealt out the money.

"Like a pack of cards." Eugenio had been shocked. "They were like wolves. They did not trust one another at all! They watched his every movement."

Thus the first deal was completed, but it turned out that the second deal could not, after all, be completed that day. None of us had known that Evaristo ought to have brought his wife with him.

"What for?" we asked.

Evaristo explained with a chuckle. "The lawyer told us that I can buy anything I like – if I have got the money, of course – but I can't sell any land without my wife's signature too."

"It seems it's a rather new law," added Eugenio. "Until recently a man could sell his farm or his woods just at the market, one day when he happened to have drunk himself silly, and his wife could do nothing about it! Not now, of course."

So, two days later, we all met in the lawyer's office. The second contract was read aloud and Robert, Evaristo and his wife signed. This time no money was exchanged, but Robert and Evaristo simultaneously tore up the two copies of their private agreement and shook hands.

At last we had reached a satisfactory end to the matter. But it turned out that this was not so! Here was another game of snakes and ladders, and this time the snake had a strange lash in its tail.

First the Land Registry in the capital lost our papers because they were moving. They found them almost a year later. Then we went to register our wood in our local Land Registry, the final step.

But no! The registrar, new and very meticulous said, "No." There was a law dating from 1914 which laid down that foreigners could not buy agricultural land within ten miles of the coast without permission from the Military Governor. We found no one who understood the reason.

We were gob-smacked! What now? The only solution the registrar could suggest was that we should sell the wood to a trusted friend, get the necessary permission, and then buy it back. And so we did.

18

Don Quixote's garden

"Traballo comenzado, medio acabado." (Gallego saying)
Work begun, half done.

Visitors to the garden in the early days will remember Robert as a very tall, pipe-puffing man, often untidily dressed, leading them round the large areas of semi-cleared hillside, which was spattered with tiny white labels, marking even tinier plants. Botanists and cognoscenti followed him closely, squatting down from time to time to examine some treasure. My job was to bring up the rear, desperately trying to prevent the followers, particularly high-heeled ladies, from stepping on the baby plants. It was on one of these occasions that I overheard someone say, "This is the English Don Quixote."

Of course there was no Rosinante, nor any damsels in distress, but this eccentric Englishman was setting out to follow his dream, apparently against all odds. Here was a neglected hillside, rough grass, gorse, whin, bracken and bramble thickets. For help he had Ernesto, a small local farmer, who was willing but with no knowledge nor experience of gardens.

I loved the place, and took a keen interest in the development of the garden, but Robert's approach to gardening was too scientific for me and I had little influence, and no memory for the Latin names of hundreds of plants. At times he was glad of my practical help and I did the larger share of dealing with bureaucracy, and with getting to know the village and its people. He was very single-minded, and with regard to his garden, a loner.

The climate and soil were very different from those of the English Midlands. The climate was Atlantic mild temperate with only occasional frosts, which drained away down the south-east facing slope. In winter the south-west winds brought in gales and very heavy rain, giving an average rainfall of sixty inches a year. The soil was acid, sandy decomposed granite, mostly rather shallow. In places, rocks stuck up through it and odd boulders, too big to move, lay about. In such a damp, mild climate a very wide range of plants from all over the world can be grown.

But the *finca* was so big – too big, commonsense would say. The plants grew fast but the weeds grew faster. Gradually, with the stubborn persistent use of modern herbicides, more and more of the expanse turned into parkland and garden.

Then there were the rabbits, magpies and pigeons, all with ancient residents' rights. Some summers there were periods of drought. Erosion too, was a problem: once the weeds were cleared from the slope, the winter rains washed out gullies before there was time to establish plants to hold the loose soil. No wonder our visitors thought Robert was trying to achieve the impossible! Sometimes I thought so too, and no doubt Ernesto did.

Robert's dream "to make a garden" was really much more. He wanted to obtain and experiment with as many plants as possible from all over the world to see what would grow at La Saleta.

Since 1969 we had been bringing plants from England on each visit, and, once we were living there, we brought more each time we visited England. Now he corresponded with Botanic Gardens and plant nurseries in many countries, and they sent him seeds to try out. He became more and more knowledgeable about plants, their families, species, and characteristics, and carried on a world-wide correspondence about their growth or failure. Very methodical, he entered every plant on a filing card with its provenance, date of planting, and fate. He bought an engraving machine and labelled them all neatly.

The first winter after our arrival, while we were living in the old house, he had some of the pines cleared from the woodland to make paths, and spaces in which to plant rhododendrons and azaleas. Then he drew up a planting plan on squared paper, with the names entered in his tiny, tidy handwriting. Many years later, I was to try and identify those that had lost their labels and found the task beyond me. The map had turned to lace and I could not read many of the names, and those I could read seemed to be growing in different places. Maybe Ernesto, who did some of the planting, had forgotten, or not understood, what he had been told. Quite apart from the language problem, it was many years before he understood what "Don Roberto" was trying to do. At first Robert was disappointed in his progress, finding it difficult to teach him, but gradually Ernesto did come to appreciate the plants, names or no names, and to feel concern for their welfare.

Much of the *finca* was already roughly terraced and, when the new house was being built, it became obvious that retaining walls were needed or the house might slide away down the hill. So Robert got the stonemasons to build these in rough, beige-grey stone to tone with the house. They used a tripod and pulley system for lifting the heavy stones like that used for building the Pyramids. They also constructed two ponds, a small one beside the house and a large one below the house. Robert wanted a system of fountains for the big pond, and carefully drew out his idea, but sadly it did not work very well and the electricity for the pumps proved too expensive.

Before leaving England we had consulted Brenda Colvin, a well-known garden designer, showing her photos of the property and asking for her advice about layout. She drew us a possible plan, which was very helpful in general, though the details were too difficult to carry out with the resources we had. Basically, the idea was to have limited formal planting of shrubs and perennials around the house, gradually giving way to informal groups of trees and shrubs down the slope and in the level area at the bottom, which was already bounded by a narrow belt of pines and eucalyptus and a stone boundary wall.

Our builders also built a small brick building for storage hut and potting shed, and behind it a concrete platform, and rectangular troughs for water with outlets and water supply. There Robert set up a mist propagation unit.

There too, he and one of our sons mounted up the metal greenhouse frame that had come, packed flat, from England with our furniture. The glass panes were bought, cut to measure, in Pontevedra and transported home in the trailer. Inevitably there were breakages because of our bumpy track and the last piece of glass, strangely shaped, had to be replaced three or four times because it was so difficult to fit. Thus Robert had facilities for quite large-scale propagation of his plants, which gave him years of interest and pleasure.

Quite early on, Robert went to visit the nearby Forestry Experimental Station and obtained much useful advice. Because the *finca* was so large, we considered making a lemon or peach plantation in the field area at the bottom. However, we were advised that the climate was not reliable enough for regular lemon production, but that peaches were a possibility. We visited a peach plantation but decided against such an ambitious idea as we had not got the resources to get started, nor indeed any clear idea of the work involved in caring for the trees, picking and marketing the fruit.

Robert planted and planted, and most of his plants grew fast, some even too fast when their roots were not well enough established in the soil, and the next gale blew them over. Some failed or got eaten by rabbits. For several years, Ernesto's afternoon work was spraying weeds – a job like painting the Forth Bridge, which he found very boring!

As the old vines were cleared away, we wondered what to do with the hundreds of granite posts. Ernesto suggested selling them and found buyers for some, but then we realised that they would make excellent edging for beds, and fit in very appropriately with the stone of house and walls.

Robert and Ernesto established a flourishing vegetable garden down the north side of the property, and also grew strawberries, raspberries and asparagus from plants brought from England. Gooseberries and blackcurrants failed, and our first crop of sweet corn, just ready to pick, was stripped overnight by the pigeons. So we didn't bother to start again.

Then there were the bees. Robert's mother had kept bees when he was a boy and he had always wanted to keep his own. So now Roderick recommended an expert who would transfer the bees from the beehive room wall into modern hives. The process was laborious and took several visits but, once accomplished, we had several good seasons until the bees went "wild". Then Robert had some new "tame" bees sent from the United States and established them over the other side of the property, and for a time we had a lot of delicious honey. However, they too must have mated with some local wild strain and they too turned "wild" and stung Ernesto especially viciously. He then developed a dangerous allergy and it was not safe to keep them.

Until recently, very little gardening had been done in Galicia. What gardens existed belonged to the *pazos* (manor houses) many of which had originally been feudal towers, and then enlarged and turned into gracious residences during the seventeenth and eighteenth centuries. They had formal gardens, with stone walls, stairways and balustrades, fountains and box hedges. Magnolias, camellias, eucalyptus and cedars had grown huge. Until the end of the nineteenth century there was much interest in gardening in upper-class circles, but their owners residing in Madrid for most of the year, political unrest and then the Civil War, had led to their neglect.

About the time we went to Galicia there was a new upsurge of interest in gardening. Nursery gardens sprang up and expanded to meet the needs of a newly prosperous middle class. Robert wrote to the owners of nearby *pazos* asking if we might visit their gardens, and the owners returned our visits. Botanists, biologists, foresters, and some members of the staff of the Madrid Botanical Garden, as well as the simply curious, came to see what this Englishman was doing, and thus we made some very good friendships.

One day Roderick brought a Spanish friend to visit us. They arrived laughing. On the way Roderick had tried to explain Robert's dream. His friend, self-taught in English exclaimed, "Ah – now I understand. He has plants in his belfry!"

Joking apart, what Robert accomplished in those first years was astonishing, because of his vision and hard work. But unlike what most of us would do, he did not begin by preparing and planting around the house and then working outwards, but planted his plants all over the *finca*, here and there, just where he thought they would like to be. Thus visitors to the garden found their surprised disbelief changing to surprised admiration, although it was only too evident how much work remained to be done. I have a little plan of the situation of trees and shrubs at some point in the early years though I have no date for it. I think it was made for the guidance of the first group visit, that of the Spanish Horticultural Society, which seemed to be made up mainly of professional plant growers and their wives from all over Spain, on a tour round Galicia. It may not have been more than a guide to the most interesting plants doing well, listing seventy-two of them, and indicating the main zones of his general plan.

Part Three

Galicia as We Knew It

19

The countryman's year

"En tempo de vendima, auga do ceo mala, pero da fonte boa."
(Gallego saying)
At grape-picking time, water from the sky is bad, but water
from the spring good.

In England we had lived in a town, and now we had special enjoyment from contact with the cycle of the year in the country, agricultural, social and religious. In Galicia the joker in the pack is the erratic Atlantic weather.

In autumn there was the grape harvest and the anxiety that accompanied it. In our district the vines were grown on trellises supported by granite posts, thus keeping the plants drier and better exposed to the sun. The wine was sour because there was not a dependable hot summer and fine autumn. Grape picking was a priority job and everyone who could took a week or so off work to pick. Whole families set out together with their carts loaded up with tubs and baskets for the day, returning in the dusk, their unlit carts a danger to motorists and to themselves.

Once the wine was safely in the barrels, a man used to come round the farms to distil the *aguardiente* (lit. burning water) from the residue of skins and pips. These men were licensed and brought their own stills, and spent a night in each farmyard tending a wood fire under the cauldron. Nowadays this no longer takes place because the spirit has to be made in government-controlled centres.

One year, not long after our arrival, the *aguardiente* man arrived in Don Maximino's farm and found no wood for his fire. The priest looked around and said, "Oh yes, there is some wood. Look! You can burn those old wooden saints we turned out of the church last year." Then he went off to bed, and the *aguardiente* man settled down in the *alpendre* beside his still and made his fire. After an hour or so, he began to hear strange noises from the outhouse the other side of the *alpendre* wall – groaning and sighing and moaning. The poor man got more and more nervous. Surely it was unwise to burn saints, however old? Perhaps their ghosts were protesting? Finally he could bear it no longer and ran into the house and knocked on the priest's bedroom door.

"Don Maximino! Don Maximino!" he called. "The spirits of the saints are complaining!"

Don Maximino got up and went down in his nightgown to see what the trouble was. There were indeed very strange noises.

"Ah, now I understand," he said. "It's all right. There is nothing to be afraid of. There is a nasty smell coming from burning old paint on those saints, and it's disturbing the cows and the hens in the stable."

There is an old tradition of making a mulled *aguardiente* when there is company sitting round the fire on cold winter evenings. The brew is called *queimada* (burnt) and here is the translation of a recipe I was given:

An earthenware pot.
An iron pan with a handle.
Aguardiente.
Lemons and sugar.

Method: Empty a carboy of *aguardiente* slowly into the pot, smoothly and continuously, accompanied by ceremonial singing. Add the peel of one lemon for each litre of *aguardiente*. Using a twig of oak as a match, set fire to the *aguardiente*. Brown a small pan-full of sugar for each litre of *aguardiente*, over a slow fire, and when it is caramelised, pour it into the *aguardiente*. Let the mixture continue to burn until the flame turns blue, which is the crucial moment when the *queimada* is ready. Put out the flame with a linen cloth spread over the whole surface of the pot. Serve the *queimada* in an earthenware cup – nice and hot.

I never tried to make it, perhaps for lack of ceremonial singers. However, just before I finally left La Saleta, a group of young people made a fire in the yard, one evening at dusk, and brewed up their version, accompanied by singing. It was very good.

After the grapes, the maize had to be got in. The cobs were stripped from stalks and sheaths in the farmyard and then stored in the *hórreo*, a small granite building, standing up from the ground on stone legs, each leg capped by a stone disk, called a *tornaratos* (to turn back rats). The wooden entrance door is in the long side of the store, and access is by a removable ladder. At each end of the gable roof there are stone ornaments, generally a cross at one end (which leads tourists to think they are tiny chapels) and at the other end a pointed cone, diamond or similar shape, believed to be a phallic symbol. Protection by both God and the Devil?

Hórreos are known to have existed for many centuries in Galicia, and in Asturias where the type is different. Not much is known about their origin except that the name must be derived from the Latin *horreum* – a barn. In a damp climate, the farmer needs a dry, well-ventilated store for his maize and potatoes, and when he needs maize flour he strips the grains from the cobs, and takes them to the mill for grinding. There were plenty of water mills for the purpose. These days maize is used as animal feed, but until after the Civil War it was made into maize bread, which itself had superseded rye bread. Wheat is now imported from Castile. The sheaths and leaves of the maize were used to stuff mattresses in the past, but now are chopped up to add to the cows' cold wet grass in winter to warm it a little. The husks were burnt on the fire, making a particularly hot fire suitable for grilling sardines.

The maize bread was baked either in a stone oven beside the *lareira* or in a communal oven somewhere in the village. Baking would be done once a week, except in poor homes, where they baked once a fortnight, an economy measure because the bread got so hard that less would be eaten, or so I was informed.

Once I was shown how the old bread ovens were used. This one was outside in the stable, and Sara, the owner, told me that the oven was heated up by burning a load of wood inside it for perhaps an hour and a half, until the stones were very hot. Then the ash and embers were thoroughly cleared out and the uncooked dough put in, and the front opening was closed with a square board, kept for the purpose. The bread was left to cook for an hour, during which time no one should open the oven. Sara told me that the traditional sponge cake, served on feast days, was baked in the same way, and that she found that she could not make one satisfactorily in her modern gas oven because too much heat came from below, and not enough from above and from the sides.

1st November, All Saints' Day, is a public holiday and a very important family and religious festival. The church bell tolls on and off all day, and there is a lot of coming and going along the roads leading to the church, as families take flowers to the graveyard and tidy up their family graves. The graveyard is a little apart from the church, surrounded by a wall. Inside the wall, all around facing inwards, are a row of family pantheons, some simple and some very ornate and ugly – to my eyes. They are rather like a chest of drawers so that each pantheon can accommodate several members of the family, in the niches. After some years in the village, I ventured to ask what happens when all the niches are full? "When the remains get really old, they crumble away and then they are taken out and placed under a stone below, which leaves room in the niches for subsequent family members," I was told, but I did not like to ask who performed this chore. Presumably the gravedigger, a little lame old man who used to call at our door once a year for a donation.

Our first year at La Saleta we went to see what happened in the cemetery in the evening of All Saints' Day. As dusk fell the families assembled, each beside their pantheon. They placed candles in glass jars with water in and lighted them, and stood there, in small groups, waiting and chatting quietly. The priest went round the pantheons praying with each family. In the space in the middle of the cemetery, little groups of small children played about, jumping and turning somersaults, but no one paid the slightest attention to them. The church bell tolled, the ropes pulled by several cheerful and noisy small boys.

When the priest had completed his round, everyone went up into the church and Mass was celebrated. The candles were left burning all night in the deserted cemetery.

As we left we met a friendly acquaintance who asked whether we had any custom like that in England. His opinion was that it was an old pagan custom, and he commented that some of the people praying most devoutly there for the souls of their forebears were not particularly interested in Christianity in their lives. We had observed for ourselves that several anti-church friends were among the crowd.

To conclude this topic, a macabre note. At this time the town patisserie shops sell *huesos de santo* (saints' bones), piling the windows high with what look like bits of meat, fried golden brown. They turn out to be like a Danish doughnut, fried and dusted with sugar. A good seasonal delicacy.

During the winter months, from November until the spring, the weather is often very wet, sometimes with weeks and weeks of wind and rain, although there are occasional grey days and wonderful, fine, sparkling ones too. It is a relatively quiet time for the farmers: their rye has been sown and the potatoes have been lifted and stored in the *hórreos* for the family to eat all winter. In the late autumn, the house pig will probably have been killed, screaming shrilly, and its flesh salted for storage, and made into sausages of various kinds. The traditional date was Saint Martin's Day and the saying goes, "Every pig has his Saint Martin's Day", but nowadays I think it depends on the convenience of the family. However, there are still many people who consider that it is essential to kill the pig when the moon is waning, in order that the salted meat should last in good condition for the year to come.

All the year round but especially in the winter, the carts go up into the woods, and pine needles and low undergrowth are raked up and brought in as bedding for the animals. In the spring, the old bedding is cleared out and taken to the fields as rich manure. Many families own a piece of woodland, but, if not, they have the right to collect this undergrowth from the woodland belonging to the *Ayuntamiento* However, in later years, because of modern fertilisers and the shortage of young people in the countryside, many of the woodlands are left uncleared, which is one of the causes of the forest fires which have been such a disaster.

Always there is the routine care of farm animals. When there is time and someone is available for the job, the cows are taken out to graze instead of being fed on cut grass in the stable. One almost never sees cows grazing alone in a field. They are taken out on a rope by one of the family, commonly a grandmother or a child, who may have a great struggle to control perhaps two cows who wish to graze in different directions. When it rains the unlucky cow-minder can be seen sheltering from the rain under an umbrella, maybe for hours and hours. Eugenio told me that he did not attend school regularly because he was needed to take out the cows.

I wondered and then asked, why the cows could not graze alone as they do in other countries. There are, it seems, several good reasons. In the first place, because of the division of land into tiny plots, the meadows available are very small indeed, and there are no fences to keep the cows from eating the neighbours' grass. Then too, I was told, cows only eat well when they can walk along, so it would be unsatisfactory to tie them to a post. Then too, as a cow is a very valuable property there is the natural fear the something could happen to her. Until recently there was the fear, very real to the superstitious countryman, that someone could "put an evil eye" on his precious animal.

However, I think there is another, more subtle reason, as even when there is a reasonable expanse of grassy field, the cows are not left alone. A friend of ours, who had spent his whole working life administering and cultivating his estate, told me that he believed it was because the Galician cow was accustomed to living close to her human owners. Traditional houses are so constructed that the animals, who live underneath the humans, are never out of earshot; being accustomed to hearing voices and shouts, one could say they are part of the family. Alone in a field then, they feel lonely and abandoned, and therefore do not eat well.

He told me that he had once bought an excellent cow from his neighbour. The animal worked hard, was manageable, but refused to feed although he took her to his best meadows. After a week, he had to return her to her previous owner and, at once, she started to feed normally again. He supposed that she had been homesick and pining for her own family.

In 1970 at Christmas, we had unusually fine, cold weather, with frost at night and sunshine by day. There was even a snowstorm, such a rare occurrence that it was the first time Ernesto had seen snow, though there is snow inland in the mountains every winter. For the single day that the snow lay on the ground, the village was paralysed and the bus failed to get up the hill.

Well before Christmas that first year, Robert started to make propaganda about buying a turkey. Now we had never seen a turkey, nor a duck or goose either, in the market or in a shop, so I consulted Aurelia of the fruit shop.

"Oh yes," she said. "You get a turkey at the street market on 15th December, but I'll have to come with you to buy one or you'll get cheated!"

As I drove home I realised that she had been talking about a live turkey, and the more I thought about it, the more sure I was that I was not willing to buy a live turkey and drive home with it in the car, let alone kill and prepare it! However, it did not come to that, as the specialist chicken shop beside the market assured me that they would have turkeys on Christmas Eve, ready for the oven, and so they did – but only on Christmas Eve. Why would anyone want it earlier?

One later year we were presented with a live turkey in a cardboard box, a couple of days before Christmas. Ernesto came to the rescue and took it home to his farm to look after and then brought it back one morning, got it very drunk by pouring *aguardiente* into its beak and then cut its throat. But he refused to help with taking off its feathers, because he said that was always his wife's work so he didn't know how to do it. It proved remarkably difficult, even after I had found some instructions in a cookery book.

We were surprised to discover that Christmas in the countryside, and in Spain as a whole, is not nearly as important as Easter. On Christmas Eve there is family feasting within homes, traditionally *bacalao* (dried salt cod) and cauliflower, followed by nuts and figs and *aguardiente*. On Christmas Day there is Mass mid-morning as on an ordinary Sunday or feast day.

In the towns the celebrations are more sophisticated. There is midnight Mass on Christmas Eve and several Masses on Christmas Day. In Pontevedra the shop windows are trimmed and decorated, nuts, figs, and crystallised fruits arranged in piles in the food shops, and *turrón* (a kind of nutty toffee). When I went to look for marzipan, I was surprised to find that it was really like a cake, layers of marzipan elaborately decorated and made up into the form of a snake, maybe curled up in a presentation box or sold by the section. In the best patisserie in Pontevedra they set up a shelf round the shop, and the marzipan snake stretched out all along it.

It is only in the last few years that Christmas trees began to appear, and the real time for gifts is Epiphany. During the previous week the towns have processions of the Three Kings who distribute sweets, and Spanish children put out their shoes on the night of 5th January for the Three Kings to fill with presents.

Thus, one way and another, the festive season lasts three weeks, and then life settles down again to its normal rhythms. The vines have to be pruned and then later the new shoots have to be tied to the trellises with young red willow shoots, pre-soaked in cold water to make them pliable.

At the end of January, our parish celebrated its Patron Saint's day with three days of special Masses and feasting in homes. One year Don Maximino invited us to lunch on the second feast day, and having entertained the priests from neighbouring parishes the previous day, he had engaged a cook to prepare both lunches. The only other guest was a priest from another parish, a lifelong friend who had been at the seminary with Don Maximino. At first both priests were shy and glum, but when well fed and wined, they cheered up and were good company. They recounted that they had started to learn French at the seminary, but this entailed going out to a teacher in the town. In theory they had permission to go, but in the event the college authorities were always making difficulties, presumably for fear they should meet girls on the way. So they had made little progress with their French.

In the cold, bare dining room with its floor of scrubbed boards, it was a memorable meal. We started at two p.m. with a dish of scallops followed by one of clams. Then came *callos* (tripe) which is a local speciality being a stew of tripe, pig's trotters, chick peas, and other unspecified ingredients – tasty but filling. After that there was boiled hake, decorated with hard-boiled eggs, followed by a dish of cold meat, rolled up round a stuffing and sliced like a Swiss roll. Then almond tart. We drank tumblerfuls of Don Maximino's own white wine, then his red, and finished up with coffee and brandy, by which time it was 5.30 p.m. I had to lie down quietly for the rest of the evening.

Then before Lent begins, comes *Carnaval*, a street occasion with, in the past, processions and dances in which the participants disguised themselves in fancy dress and wore masks. In Eugenio's youth there were great goings-on, he told me. The young men used to go around playing practical jokes on their neighbours, and it was considered very funny, for example, to take gates off their hinges and hide them in the woods. After the Civil War, people became "better behaved" and the wilder practices lapsed. The Church, supported strongly by the Franco regime, disapproved and stamped on many of the old customs. After Franco died, the old celebrations began reappearing, with processions and parties and disguised children going round the houses asking for carnival money – a version of "trick or treat", in fact.

Towards the end of February there are the first signs of spring. As soon as the soil dries up a little, there is a great rush of work in the fields: ploughing, spreading manure and planting onions, garlic and potatoes. The frogs start to croak on warmer nights and the first crickets to chirp.

All over Spain, Easter is the most important religious festival of the year. Palm Sunday is the start, when specially prepared palm branches are sold and taken to Mass to be blessed. In Galicia, there are no palms so it is not palms but olive branches, and after Mass they are taken home and hung up over the house or stable door to protect the farm from thunder and lightning. On Holy Thursday, candles are taken to the church and lighted, and blessed by the priest, and left burning in the church till Good Friday, when each person or family takes their candle home to keep all the year, and to light in times of severe illness or emergency. In towns in Holy Week, very elaborate processions are held every afternoon, and some parishes put on Passion plays.

One ancient custom still existed when we arrived. Each household brought a dozen eggs as an Easter offering to the priest, bachelors and widows just half a dozen; the priest then sold them to make a little extra income. A special Easter bread is baked and godparents present it to their godchildren, as also bread "nests" containing eggs – very hard as they are baked with the bread.

As in England, April is a beautiful month; the oaks burst into leaf, and the fruit trees blossom. The grass is a rich emerald green, studded with wild flowers, and the pine trees flower, throwing up pinkish-red candle-shaped tips to their branches and giving off a fine, slightly sticky, greenish-yellow pollen which got in my eyes and made it impossible for me to wear my contact lenses.

The first of May, like carnival, used to have a whole range of presumably pagan traditions, now almost lost. Still, however, some of the villagers pinned branches of golden-flowering whin to their doors, to ward off the evil eye. We wondered how it was that May Day was a public holiday in Franco's Spain and the explanation was curious. In Republican times, the first of May was celebrated as Socialist Workers' Day, and the political aspect merged easily with the traditional. Franco suppressed the festival until, as part of a loosening up of policies, it was once more permitted semi-disguised as the feast of *San José Obrero* (Saint Joseph the Worker). Thus Saint Joseph, whose day is really 19th March, got an extra day as a carpenter, which sanctified Workers' Day and the pagan May Day at the same time.

May is a busy month. The maize is sown in shallow trenches, which are filled in and then banked up and kept carefully weeded. In July and August it must be watered, a heavy and tiring job. The system of water rights is ancient and complicated. Some farms have their own water, but, if not, a little stream or spring belongs to several families who each have their dates and times to use it. Ernesto explained to me that his land was in two parts. One part had water rights during the month of July, for one day from nine a.m. till nine p.m. and one night from nine p.m. till nine a.m. The other part had water one day from eleven a.m. till eleven p.m. and one night from eleven p.m. till eleven a.m. Until 1950, nothing in his village had been written down about these rights but in that year the local *Juez de la Paz* wrote it all down and gave each family a document setting out their rights.

The procedure is this: as the water flows in its little runnel into the maize field, the farmer or his wife have to ensure that it runs up and down between all the rows of half-grown plants. They use their mattocks to scoop out the soil, opening up a channel here and closing another one there, so their turn means staying all the hours to attend to the proper flowing of the precious water.

The moveable Church festival of Corpus Christi generally falls in June and is a public holiday in Spain. The occasion is celebrated in the village on one of the Sundays near the date, so that the priests of neighbouring parishes can join in conducting a sung Mass in each of their churches in turn. In Don Maximino's time it was one of the rare occasions that he allowed a procession, and the Host was carried out down the flight of stone steps in front of the church to a shrine, set up beneath the stone cross which stands there. The shrine consisted of a little shelter with a carpet on the ground, altar with flowers, candles and some embroidered cushions, and flower petals were strewn all along the route of the procession up the steps to the church door. In some places the carpet of flowers for the procession has become an elaborate work of art, worked on all the previous night. The *fiesta* is announced the previous evening, and, in the morning, by the usual salvos of rockets, and, during the morning, the bagpipers beat the bounds of the parish. Mass starts and hearty though melancholy singing floats out of the packed church, and eventually the untidy procession flows out: candlestick bearers, children having celebrated their first Communion in white dresses and suits, the priest under a canopy borne by half a dozen parishioners, the other priests, and behind, the rest of the congregation. They move slowly down the steps to the shrine, kneel there and pray and sing, and then the procession reforms and returns to the church, where the service continues for another ten minutes. Finally, everyone streams out into the sunshine to the skirl of bagpipes and the banging of rockets.

Corpus Christi is a truly Christian festival but Saint John's Eve is pagan, a vestige of the old Midsummer Night, celebrated with a dance in the market place and with bonfires, which young couples jump over to ensure fertility. In 1971, one of the workers on our new house brought us a plastic bag filled with flowers and leaves, mint, thyme, honeysuckle, marguerites and various other strong, sweet-smelling leaves. He instructed us to put all these in a bucket of water, which we should leave out overnight "to see the face of the moon". Next morning we should wash in this fragrant water. We did as we were told, and the water was indeed fragrant, but I am not sure what the resulting benefit was – or should have been.

That year we had our own private Saint John's Eve omen – if such it was – when a little owl fell down the chimney suddenly at dusk. This was a fluffy young bird, who allowed me to pick him up and take him outside where he flew away uncertainly. A beautiful white owl used to nest in the dovecote. We used to hear these owls calling at night, and were told that when the old women heard this cry at night they would say that someone had died.

Fine summer evenings had a special glory if we sat on our terrace into the dark. The sun went early from our garden because of the hill behind the house, but it lit up the ranges of hills across the valley, highlighting them in a pink and orange glow. The moon rose over the shoulder of our nearest mountain. Sitting quietly and listening, one noticed how many noises there were: crickets buzzing and birds singing, clucking or squeaking; the frogs in the pond with their solo and chorus croaking. Across the valley lorries climb the hill or blare their horns; a noisy motorbike roars on its way; dogs bark and cows moo and the crows have noisy arguments. And, down in the fields, people still working shout to each other or to their animals.

In August, workers on the land find themselves with some free time and the small bus-owner in the village used to run an afternoon bus to the beach. And of course every village has its summer *fiesta*, which, since Franco's restraining influence had gone, has become bigger and noisier with dancing going on into the early hours of the morning. The more noise the better, so that all the neighbouring villages shall know that this is a splendid affair. I think the Galicians like noise.

20

Religion and the Church

"Fai o que o crego dixere e non o que fixere." (Gallego saying)
Do what the priest said not what he did.

Religion plays an important, even central, part in the life of country people in Galicia, in the personal sense and also because of the strength and power of the Church. As outsiders, we were observers and so I can only comment on those aspects of this role which interested us and which we could attempt to understand.

The tangible signs of Christianity are all around. The parishes are small and their church is nearly always built on the side of the hill that overlooks the cultivated valley, thus presiding over the numerous hamlets of the parish. Unlike Castile where the villagers live in concentrated villages surrounded by their fields, in Galicia the population is scattered around in single farmhouses or small groups of houses among the fields. The churches are small, grey stone buildings, generally Romanesque in style with baroque facades, many of them very old, or rebuilt with the same materials and style. Parish boundaries are known to have been almost unaltered since their establishment, perhaps as early as the fifth century AD.

As the church can be seen, so can its bell, generally a bit cracked, be heard from everywhere, summoning to Mass, tolling a death, or, in emergencies, calling out the people to combat the danger. "What is that smoke?" or "Who is the bell tolling for?" – single peals for a man, double for a woman, or is it the other way round?

As in Ireland and Brittany, there are stone crosses at road and path intersections. A common model has the figure of Christ on the Cross and below, smaller, the serpent, and Adam and Eve anxiously holding fig leaves over their private parts. A plain cross by the roadside marks the spot where someone met with a violent death, generally during the Civil War.

The festivals of the Church punctuate the year: Christmas, Palm Sunday, Easter, Corpus Christi and the principal Saints' days. Besides their religious importance, they have practical significance. *San Martín* is the time to kill the pig and also to sample the new season's wine – a suitable accompaniment to the rare treat of fresh pork for dinner. In our district, the maize should be sown after *San Marcos* (25th April) and the vines sprayed for the second time between *San Antonio* (13th June) and *San Pedro* (29th June) and the rye harvested after *San Pedro* – a sort of rural calendar.

There are special virtues attributed to particular saints: *San Marcos* will care for your rheumatism and *San Bartolomé* will cure children of nightmares; *Santa Marta* has a special interest in earache and snake bites. Near us there was a well attended Mass each year on the day of *San Blas*, patron saint of throats, who will perhaps cure your sore throat and help you if you choke. *San Cristóbal*, patron saint of travellers, was downgraded one year, I suppose by the Pope. That year the young bloods of the village had organised a procession of cars and lorries. When a car ran into a lorry, the doctor joked, "What do you expect? If *San Cristóbal* is downgraded, how can he protect you?"

The Galicians are believed to be of mainly Celtic stock, and they attribute many of their characteristics to these forebears, such as their deep attachment to certain shrines – for example those at springs, oak groves and hill tops – to Celtic pantheism. When the Romans conquered the country they took over many of these same places for the worship of their gods, and subsequently the early Christians did likewise, endowing each suitably with a titular saint, to which was added, if not already in existence, the tradition of a miracle. Christian and pagan beliefs are thus inextricably entangled.

Death draws the village community very close together. When someone dies the neighbours go to call at the house almost at once "to keep the family company". The family of the dead person and others may sit up all night with the corpse, watching and praying. The funeral will be the following day, and all the neighbours escort the coffin from the house to the church in a silent walking procession, led by the priest.

We were confused by the remarkable number of funerals that passed the house. Surely there could not be so many deaths? Then someone managed to explain that what we call a funeral is an *entierro* (burial) and that the Spanish word, *funeral,* meant an anniversary Mass, celebrated after one year and often after subsequent years too.

An English friend of ours, a lonely widower and not a Catholic, died in his village, and the villagers turned out to escort his coffin to the cemetery, led by the priest. Then the priest stood aside and the British Consul said a few prayers and the coffin was placed in one of the niches belonging to the Englishman's drinking friend, the builder.

There was a sad sequel to this event. The Englishman had left a small legacy to his friend, who then took to drinking himself useless, until, fortunately, the money was all spent, when he pulled himself together and went back to building.

I think it would be true to say that in our early years in Galicia the majority of the villagers were fundamentally religious, and many of the women, especially, very devout indeed, imbued with a deep sense of the mystery of life and of the presence, not too far away, of God, Jesus, the Virgin and the saints.

Beside the strong preoccupation with death and with the after-life, legends of ghosts and visitations abounded, believed by some, half-believed by others. However, there were certainly individuals – and I cannot guess how many – who were anti-Church, though, because of social pressures or simply from habit, they might comply with their Church's minimum requirements.

In the past the Church was very powerful. Until the disestablishment of the monasteries and the appropriation by the state of their land in 1836, the Church was the biggest landowner in Galicia with feudal powers over the lives of its tenants. There were innumerable monasteries with their dependent priories and farms, some dating from the earliest Christian settlements from the fifth century onwards, and others, probably the majority, dating from the heyday of the great pilgrimages to Santiago de Compostela in the twelfth to fifteenth centuries. After the disestablishment of the monasteries, the hold on land and thus the practical power of the Church was lessened, but nevertheless there remained considerable moral pressure, the weight of tradition, and, of course, the deeply rooted faith of the people. During the 1930s, in contrast to what happened in many other parts of Spain, it seems that there was no strong wave of feeling against the Church, priests, monks and nuns. But the Franco regime strongly supported the Church as a traditional and powerful authoritarian force for law and order, and thus church and state worked together to suppress any upsurge of independent or revolutionary thinking, or the infiltration of new ideas.

We were told that once a year during Lent, the priest used to read out in church a list of the names of all those who had not confessed during the year, so that their families should bring pressure to bear on them to do so – "so of course we all went – but we did not tell the truth".

In those times too, when applying for many jobs, especially in service of the state or applying for a scholarship, it was necessary to produce not only a certificate of baptism but also a letter, signed by the local mayor, testifying that you were a person of good conduct. If the priest vetoed you, there was no appeal. It was hardly surprising that most people avoided thinking about matters which might be considered dangerous, and those who were critical of church or state kept their mouths shut, or resorted to cynicism and entertained themselves and their trusted friends with funny stories belittling or making fun of those in high places or of their village representatives.

An example: "One day the sacristan went to confession and the priest asked him, 'Who goes round helping himself to the money in the Church collecting boxes?' The sacristan answered, 'I'm sorry, I can't hear you very well.' So the priest repeated his question and the sacristan said, 'No, out here I can't hear anything you say.' The priest said, 'Of course you can – look here – we'll change places and I shall be able to hear perfectly.' So the sacristan went inside the confessional box and the priest knelt down outside and the sacristan said, 'Who is it that runs after my wife? Who is it who keeps following her around?' 'You're quite right,' said the priest, 'one can't hear anything out here!'"

The village priest plays an essential role in the tight-knit web of village life, which is now breaking down as more and more of the parishioners work away from the village. He is respected, highly respected in most cases, in spite of such tales as the one above, because of his celibacy or perhaps in spite of it? I don't know. A great deal of his personal influence stems from the fact that he not only lives in the village but is also a farmer depending, like everyone else, on the vagaries of the weather and the success or failure of his crops. In earlier times his living depended on his farm and parish tithes, and on charges for funerals, baptisms, weddings, et cetera; now he has a stipend from the state, but the farm is still an important part of his livelihood. So he has strong bonds of common interest even with his less devout parishioners, and he understands their lives and problems, except, of course, in the matter of marriage and parenthood.

Now everyone knows that Catholic priests are celibate, but in the Galician countryside, not everyone believes that they are. A priest has to have a woman to housekeep for him, often his mother, sister or niece, but it has come about in the course of time that the word *sobrina* (niece) has acquired a secondary meaning for the down-to-earth countryman. Eugenio told me that there was a priest of a parish some miles away who had two *sobrinas*, who took it in turns to share his bed. When I said I did not believe such a tall story, Eugenio said, "Yes, of course they do. After all, it is the man who gives the orders."

In this connection, Gerald Brenan says in his book *The Spanish Labyrinth*, first published in 1945, "In the Middle Ages it was established custom, permitted by the bishops, for Spanish priests to have concubines. They wore a special dress and had special rights and were called *barraganas*. When the Council of Trent forbade this practice to continue, the Spanish clergy protested. In fact they have never paid much attention to the prohibition, for they continue to have 'housekeepers' and 'nieces' to this day. Their parishioners, far from being shocked, prefer them to live in concubinage, as otherwise they would not always care to let their womenfolk confess to them…to my knowledge it was often true until a few years ago." Probably it is no longer true, but the legend remains.

Nowadays there is a great shortage of young men wishing to enter the priesthood. Once it was the opportunity for the clever son of a poor family to get an education and a future with status, and the traditional job for the second son of an aristocratic family. Now there are so many other ways to get on in the world, and the question of celibacy adds to the problems.

When we arrived, Don Maximino was already an elderly man, tired and in poor health, a kind but limited man. He retired around 1985 and his place was taken by Don José Antonio who was already priest of the next parish and now found himself running three parishes. A very hard-working, more modern man, he enlivened the whole situation, making friends with the young people, organising outings and even excursions to the shrine at Fatíma in Portugal.

Very musical, he started an excellent choir, which came to sing at our chapel *fiesta* when he took over the Mass in later years.

When we had bought the La Saleta property we were surprised but not alarmed to find ourselves the owners of a chapel. It was in poor condition but very much cherished by the people and we were aware of the responsibility of owning it, but also aware of the irony of the situation. We were not Catholics nor even truly believers. Robert's family were Unitarians and my father-in-law would have been upset at even the idea that we could own a chapel. But we felt ourselves to be the custodians of a small, valuable, piece of Galician culture.

9 *Eugenio.*

10 *Eugenio and Celina.*

11 Ernesto.

12 Julio.

13 Robert Gimson.

14 Margaret Gimson.

15 *New house.*

16 Greenhouse and potting shed.

17   View across the valley.

18 Big lily pond.

19 Small pond from new house veranda.

21

Women's lives

"A muller que malla no home, fai ben, si pode." (Gallego saying)
A woman who beats the man does well, if she can.

When the Romans marched into Galicia in the second century BC, they were opposed by the fierce warlike tribes of the region. It is recorded that the Celtic women fought alongside their men, preferring if defeated, to kill themselves and their children rather than become Roman captives.

This tough physical and mental independence has endured throughout the centuries, and, to this day, the Galician women play a full and equal part in the life of the countryside. They have equal inheritance rights and work in the fields alongside the men, carrying on alone if they are widowed or if their men are away. When the men are at home, there do seem to be certain usual divisions of the workload. We saw the men pruning the vines, tying them up, and later spraying them, but the grape-picking is done by the whole family. The women take their produce to market but it is mainly the men who trade in cows, sheep, goats and pigs. Chickens, their rearing, care and the sale of surplus eggs, seem to be the responsibility of the women. In the evenings it is the men who go to the bar, to play cards, watch television, and discuss the affairs of the village.

Thus the Galician country women are very different from those of other parts of Spain. They seem hardly to cultivate their personal beauty, once past first youth. Their skins harden and wrinkle from exposure to sun and wind, and they pull their hair back and tie a triangular headscarf on tightly over it, well down over their foreheads to just about eyebrow level, knotting the ends behind their heads. During our early years in the village, all married women wore black, a dress or skirt and blouse with an apron over it, boots for working in the fields and, in summer, a wide-brimmed straw hat. Now, of course, there is colour in their dress, and jeans are worn by all the younger women. We were interested to find that the women were more outgoing, prepared to talk to us, openly curious and more informative than many of the cautious, suspicious men. An amusing characteristic of the Galician is that they prefer not to answer a question directly, often responding with a question of their own, which, for me, turned into a game that two can play.

Compared with other rural areas in Spain, there were very few crafts practised, presumably because the women worked outside. I used to go and talk to Manuel de la Rochela who was born in 1906 and had a very good memory. He told me he remembered the cultivation of flax, which had a strange smell "like the fat that runs out of sardines". The women used to tease the fibres and then roll them between their fingers to make thread: "this could be done while minding cows". Specialist houses still did weaving when he was a boy, for themselves and for others, making sheets, tablecloths, et cetera. And he remembered some women making crochet bedspreads, but otherwise there was no tradition of sewing, embroidery, or knitting. There was some basket-making inland, and brown earthenware crockery made from time immemorial in places where suitable clay was found, but these were small workshop industries rather than cottage crafts. In the fishing villages of La Coruña province there is still lace-making of a very high standard.

The average farmhouse was small, barely furnished with beds, a table and chairs, a sideboard and maybe a storage chest. The only warm place was beside the kitchen fire, until the arrival early in the century of wood-burning iron stoves, and then gas stoves, the gas supplied from orange cylinders delivered around the villages once a week. In the last ten to fifteen years, central heating has arrived in better-off houses, as have bathrooms.

As for cooking, apart from *caldo Gallego* (the basic soup-stew), the local dishes of repute were for special occasions: little and sweet pancakes for Carnival, *empanadas* (pies) for *romerías*, *bacalao* (dried salt cod) for

Christmas and a thick cake-like rice pudding to round off a fiesta lunch. Then there was a rich tradition of folk songs, dances, and bagpipe music. Galician museums preserve beautiful and varied *fiesta* costumes but in our village no one remembered owning one, even as an heirloom. Now they have re-appeared with the revival of interest in local folklore, stimulated by the government to encourage tourism and promote Galician nationalism.

In spite of the considerable independence of the Galician women, courting customs seemed to us very restrictive, though I imagine this was the case in all rural societies. The Civil War and the subsequent period of hardship and hunger, together with the cold hand of the Franco regime, seems to have added restrictions. Eugenio told me that in his young days, courting was much more free and easy. Then there were dances in the village every Sunday, and, if a young man fancied a girl, he accompanied her home and talked to her at the doorway until her parents called her in. He would go to the house and talk to her other evenings too, and so might several other young men. A lot of the girls got pregnant and perhaps their young men married them or perhaps not. However, he said too that a girl who was jilted by her young man was considered "soiled goods", and no longer marriageable, and a widow was not expected to marry again.

Manuel de la Rochela's account of his courting was a little different. His family and hers had some status in the village, higher than that of Eugenio's.

"I was married in 1929 when I was twenty-three and so was she. That was very young. We sat by the stone table in the yard to talk and we were always supervised closely by her mother or by the maid. Young people met at *fiestas* and could talk freely then, but only one young man would come to the house to court the girl. He was the *novio* [fiancé]. When the young couple decided to get married, his parents would come to ask for the girl's hand for their son and certainly, in most cases, it was the young couple who decided. They might have to wait a long time, until the young man was able to marry, that is until he had done his military service – three years it was then – and had a livelihood."

The fact that there are so many unmarried mothers in the countryside suggests that, even with all this care, there are many opportunities for more intimate meetings between young people. No doubt it is for this reason that the need to take care of their reputation is drilled into the young women – and not only the young women are worried about this.

Once when I was away, leaving Robert alone in the house, he fell ill and ran a high temperature. The doctor came to see him and said he should not be alone in the house for the night. María-Ester was coming in every evening to cook his meal, and Robert asked her if she would sleep in the house that night. The answer was "No! That would be very *feo* [ugly]." Her mother, Celina, would not consider it either and the only solution would have been to ask Eugenio to come. Later we made enquiries about this, and general opinion, corroborated by the doctor himself, was that it was quite normal though he thought it was an exaggerated precaution since María-Ester had worked for us for several years.

I think there are remnants of old fears mixed in with the logical care for the woman's reputation. Galicia was more or less feudal until relatively recently, at least in the attitudes of the well-to-do landowner and the peasant farmer. No doubt too there were abuses of the servant girls by the young men of the "big house" and neither the girls or their parents would have had any redress. Novels about Galicia bear this out. It is also said that there were priests who demanded "first-night rights" from the young women they married in their churches – long ago obviously, but such historical beliefs die hard. We were probably very naïve not to have realised this.

If a man and a woman are not safe together in the same house, it is a two-way danger unless they are brother and sister, or married to each other. An elderly bachelor friend of ours told me that he would like to find a married couple to keep house for him, but, so far, he had been unsuccessful. He did not want a housekeeper because: "an old woman would be incapable and no use, and a young one would expect to serve for everything."

In 1974, María-Ester got engaged and married. The young man had no family farm to inherit so the young couple settled down in the house with Eugenio and Celina. This is what María-Ester wanted anyway as she stood to inherit the farm.

The pattern of events was the traditional one. The banns were called and Eugenio and Celina entertained both families to lunch, a party of twenty-seven people including children, who sat down to a four-course meal, laid on at a day's notice by Celina and her elder daughter, Carmen. Three days later the "return match" took place when the young man's family held a similar lunch party at which details of the wedding were discussed.

During the next few days Eugenio was very distraught, trying to decide where to hold the wedding reception. There were two basic alternatives: at home, in the old style, or in a restaurant which is the new style. The reception after Carmen's wedding, ten years previously, had been at home with a cook and helpers working for several hours beforehand, cooking on an open fire in the yard, and serving the meal in the *alpendre*. But now it was much more difficult to get helpers, time was short, and anyway Eugenio decided, it would be too much for Celina. So a bar or restaurant, but where? He was counting on up to a hundred guests and it had to be a proper feast. He considered one restaurant after another and said they were all bad, expensive and bad! Eventually, accompanied by his nephew Arturo, who himself kept a small bar, he went to negotiate with the Casa Rosita and booked with them at a cost of 550 pesetas a head – a lot at that time.

All those days Eugenio rode to and fro on his horse, making the arrangements. The relations had to be invited and some of them lived some way away, though it was easy to invite the immediate neighbours. Arrangements had to be made with the priest and photographer, and the civil ceremony booked.

On Wednesday, 9th January, the young couple attended the civil marriage ceremony in the *Ayuntamiento* in the village, then they went to Pontevedra to confession – José-Luis not having confessed for eight years, they were embarrassed at the idea of the local priest knowing this!

Thursday, 10th January was a very wet day. The ceremony was to be at one o'clock and at eleven-thirty the dressmaker came to the house to dress the bride. Apart from the bride and groom, the main actors in a Spanish wedding are the *madrina* and *padrino* (literally "the godparents of the marriage"); in this case the *madrina* was María-Ester's actual godmother and I think this is usually so. The *madrina* had to go and fetch the bridegroom from his house, and the *padrino*, José-Luis's stepfather, had to fetch the bride and escort her to the church. Various other relatives had to be fetched, many of them by taxi, and a bus had to be provided to take the guests from the church to Cambados for the reception.

We did not go to the ceremony, but we went to see the company come out of church. Fortunately there was a pause in the rain, and photographs were taken and then we drove Eugenio and Celina to Cambados so they could be ahead of their guests. The young couple went by taxi.

The Casa Rosita specialised in wedding receptions and the far end of the restaurant was used, set out with two long parallel tables, with the top table for the immediate family set at a right angle at one end. Except for those at the top table, everyone sat as they pleased. The majority of the guests were in their best black clothes that they use for every important occasion, though there were a few smart young things. María-Ester wore a long white dress and small veil, José-Luis looked really smart, and Celina and Eugenio looked almost as usual. The *madrina* wore a splendid headdress made of a built-up framework with a little lacy black veil hanging from it.

About half-past two the company, about eighty-five of us, sat down to lunch. We had:

- ♦ Hors d'oeuvres consisting of small dishes of ham and sausage.
- ♦ Shellfish: first little crabs, then *centolla* (spider crab), then shrimps, then a hot dish of clams, followed by scallops – that is five different kinds served consecutively.
- ♦ Fish: fried hake (curiously enough to our ideas, no other kind of fish would do for an important occasion).
- ♦ Meat: roast veal served in slices. No accompaniments.
- ♦ Sweets: *brazo de gitano* (gypsy's arm, which is like an English Swiss roll), ice-cream and wedding cake – also served consecutively.
- ♦ Coffee and brandy.

There was a lot of coming and going around the room during the meal; people went off to the toilet or crossed the room to talk to their friends, and the many children milled around. Jokes were bandied to and fro, sadly lost on us, being entirely in Gallego. At intervals a chanted chorus, which had to be explained to us, started up, calling on the bride and groom, and the parents and godparents to kiss – considered somewhat risqué in those days as kissing had never been permitted in public between the sexes.

We left at about half past five as soon as we had had our coffee, and the party went on, we were told, until nearly seven o'clock, well sustained by many glasses of brandy. When we left the table, the whole company stood up – a gesture of respect which embarrassed us considerably.

José-Luis had wanted to go for a honeymoon trip to Madrid to stay with an aunt, or even as far as Vigo, but María-Ester refused to leave home, no, not for a single night! So they settled down at once in her home.

Once a village girl was married, she was not expected to go out alone or even to the cinema. José-Luis went to work in Barcelona for some months but María-Ester would not consider accompanying him. I think that after her marriage her whole attitude to the farm altered; now it was partly hers and the good of *la casa* (the house – almost "the family") came first.

The costs of a village wedding were enormous in relation to the means of these families, but there was another side of the equation. Guests were expected to give presents worth at least the cost of their meal, sometimes in money. This made attendance an expensive matter, and also meant that the guests were affronted if they did not receive what they considered their due – a really good meal of exactly the type they were expecting. There had to be plenty of shellfish, and hake, and we knew that Javier of the Casa Rosita had driven some thirty miles to the other side of the *ría* to obtain the shellfish for María-Ester's wedding because the bad weather had caused a scarcity. Otherwise, of course, "people would talk". Thus hosts and guests were caught up in a vicious circle of "keeping up with the Joneses", as happens elsewhere.

The money to pay for a wedding was generally raised by cutting down some pine trees. His piece of woodland served as the peasant's bank, and the growing trees gave a rate of interest that compared favourably with most other forms of investment. At that time there had been a savings bank in the village for some years, but as Eugenio explained:

"I keep money in it, but I would never borrow for a wedding, nor to build a house or buy land – only for trading in cows. You have to pay interest on the loan each three months and if you needed to borrow in the first place, how would you have money in three months' time for the interest? There used to be private money-lenders and then your farm was the security, and of course there were people who could not pay, so the money-lender got rich. I keep my spare cash in a tin box, tin against the damp, buried under my wine cellar floor."

We were told that this, at best munificence and at worst ostentation, in the matter of weddings was a relatively new development. Forty years earlier, some twenty people had attended the wedding of Don Francisco, in our time head of the new village school, but certainly there were some big weddings then too. Manuel de la Rochela told me about his:

"My wife's family kept the inn and my mother-in-law was well-known for miles around for the excellence of her cooking. My wife had the same skill. We had a huge wedding here in this house and yard. We were both from big families and the priest, who was a close friend of my parents-in-law, even brought some of his friends too, some of the gentry."

Some years after María-Ester's wedding there was one at a neighbouring farm at which two hundred guests sat down to lunch in the *alpendre*, which was extended to double its size by a tarpaulin. In this case both bride and groom came of very large families and the guests were almost all relatives. A second lunch was held next day for the neighbours and friends who could not be invited on the day itself.

This bride, Socorrito, was a most attractive and accomplished girl and was engaged for about four years. The bridegroom came from a village some miles away and was the son of a relatively well-off farmer. "It's a farm with machinery to do everything," María-Ester told me, "and they want Socorrito to go and live over there, but her family want him to come and live here because they need her help at home. So the negotiations have only been getting on very slowly." Socorrito's family lost the tug-of-war and I have no doubt she was sadly missed at home.

And after the wedding? How much did the lack of privacy in the home inhibit them, I wonder? How difficult was it for the one who came from elsewhere to settle down as a full member of the new family? How often were there good relationships between the various members of three-generation households and how often not? In the country, marriages must always have been, first and foremost, working partnerships, strong and satisfactory if both partners played their full part and enjoyed a sufficient measure of personal compatibility.

The Catholic Church has never sanctioned birth control, but around the 1980s, birth control clinics started to appear and the pill became available. For some years previously it was obtainable on a very small scale "under the counter" if you were well enough informed and could find out which counter. We knew a Dutch couple who had a Great Dane bitch and went to their local chemist when she was on heat, for a deodorant spray available in Holland. The chemist was puzzled and said no, he had never heard of such a thing but "couldn't we give her the pill we give the girls?"

I have been describing how such matters were in a country village, the one which we knew, more than thirty years ago now, and there have been very great changes since then – in every aspect of life. Recently I had news of the wedding of a young man from a family with no particular status. A friend wrote: "We went to Mercedes's son's wedding. What a country wedding! American white limousine included. *Marisco* (Shellfish) galore. Mercedes in long emerald dress and a hat and shoes to match. Wedding started at eleven a.m. followed by lunch – we got up from the table at seven-thirty – and later dance at the local disco... . What a change in Gallego rural society!"

22

Education

"Fartase de comer e de beber, pro non de saber." (Gallego saying)
One can have a surfeit of food and drink, but not of
knowledge.

Within months of our arrival in Galicia, I was asked whether I would
teach English to our architect's wife, and that led to my acquiring a
small number of adult pupils over the years. I found this of great interest
because of the stimulus and contact with people of different ages and
backgrounds, and I made firm friendships with some of them. I had no
direct qualification to teach, but a degree in French, and a little
experience from a voluntary experiment in England in the 1960s, to
teach English to some of the immigrant Indian women, and from a
couple of years working as a home teacher of children who could not
get to school for health reasons. Sadly, I managed to teach very little to
this first pupil, partly because she was from Andalusia, where they talk
at breakneck speed and drop the consonants at the end of syllables, and
she could not get her tongue around the English language. She was
very talkative and impatient as well, and I did not really understand
what she said in any language. I found too that I did not know sufficient
English grammar to explain it, but my next pupil fortunately did. She
taught me a lot of Spanish in return and subsequently helped us with
translations and other problems, and still is my very good friend. I bought
myself an English grammar book and studied it, and then I was better
prepared.

Later on, parents in the village started to bring me their children, asking for help with English, and this developed into more or less regular Saturday morning classes, often three groups of four or five children, several of whom went on to study English at university, and have remained in touch with me. Such contacts gave me a much greater understanding of the social scene and of people's lives.

In 1970 there were a dozen or more small primary schools in the district. Each parish had a state school providing primary education for the children from six to fourteen years old. In some parishes there were two, one for the boys and one for the girls. The school-leaving age had just been raised from twelve to fourteen that year. Besides these, there were a number of small private schools providing the same education in the same conditions: one teacher teaching perhaps thirty or forty children of all ages in one classroom. Normal school hours were from nine-thirty a.m. till twelve-thirty a.m. and from three p.m. till five p.m.

Manuel de la Rochela told me about earlier times: "I went to school in the village [circa 1912 to 1918]. All the boys in the parish went to the boys' school, perhaps fifty of them. We only learnt very little: to read and write and multiply. My brother learnt more because the Galicians who had emigrated to Buenos Aires sent back money to set up schools called *laicos* (lay) because no religion was taught in them, and he went there. These schools were closed by the Franco regime.

"The village schoolmaster lodged in our house. He was only a substitute as the real one was an invalid, but he still kept the job. The substitute came from near Lugo. He was paid twenty-five pesetas a month, which was a pittance even in those days. His shirts were so worn that I remember my mother telling the girl not to rub too hard in case they fell to bits."

(It helps to understand the value of twenty-five pesetas a month that an old woman told me that she had worked as agricultural labourer on our *finca*, before she married in 1910, for one peseta a day.)

At ten years old, after four years' schooling, very clever children could move to the state secondary schools in the town, but there were not a lot of places and it was rare for a village child to achieve this. A few better-off or ambitious parents moved their children to fee-paying schools in the town. The remaining children continued to attend the village schools for another four years.

The secondary schools provided four years of study leading to the *Bachillerato Elemental* at about fourteen, and another two leading to the *Bachillerato Superior*. Children going on to the university studied another year, and if they passed the exam at the end of it, were eligible to enter any university. To take a teacher training course it was necessary to have the *Bachillerato Superior*.

In 1970 Spain passed an Education Reform Act that ushered in a period of great change. With the help of the World Bank, new primary schools were built all over Galicia – all the same in design and materials – to provide primary education for all the children from six to fourteen.

In the new schools the eight *cursos* (years of study) were entitled *Educación General Básica, EGB* for short. On passing the exams of the 8th *curso,* the child obtained the certificate of *Graduado escolar,* a school-leaving certificate. Then he could transfer to one of the state secondary schools. If the child failed the 8th *curso* he stayed on until sixteen and was then given a certificate of school attendance.

The secondary schools provided three *cursos* leading to the new-style *Bachillerato,* followed, as previously, by a further year of study for those wishing to enter university. The universities then instituted new entrance procedures: each holds its own selection exams for those young people who are eligible, thus limiting the number of its students to the number it is able to teach, in theory anyway. Among the selection exams there is a compulsory English exam, not very difficult but an important hurdle for many.

The curriculum, hours and term dates were laid down by the Ministry of Education in Madrid for all the schools of Spain, although as far as dates were concerned the Director of Education for each province had the right to vary them to suit the particular local climate. The children moved up their schools *curso* by *curso* and there was no possibility for a clever child to skip a *curso.* More than that, the marks for each year were entered in a book that recorded the whole of each child's education in detail, and the resulting score affected their access to the university. A child who failed the June exam for the year, in any subject, had to retake that subject or subjects in September. If he still failed two, he could carry them forward and take them again in February, but if he failed three he had to repeat the whole *curso*. The result was that the slower children took it as normal to have to spend their summer holidays swotting up the subjects they found difficult, often at special paying classes laid on by the same teachers who had failed them. How often did these teachers need the extra money and therefore took care that a certain number of children failed?

In our district the new school opened in 1973, swallowing up all the existing small schools in the area. The teachers of these small schools were all given posts in the new school, and had to attend crash courses during the summer holidays to prepare them for the changes in the curriculum and for changes in teaching methods. Crash courses were also provided for teachers who wished to be "specialists" in various subjects including science, art and languages, which were to be taught to the older pupils. Previously French had been taught in secondary schools, but now the primary schools could choose between English and French and German, ours chose English. The staff were allocated by the Director of Education for the province, new ones only in September when the new term was ready to begin.

Advance planning for opening day was made yet more difficult by the fact that no headmaster was appointed until almost the last moment. The staff of the school voted for the three teachers they thought most suitable, and the names went to the Director of Education in Pontevedra, who selected the one he thought best, probably but not necessarily, the one with the most votes. His choice then had to be ratified by the Ministry of Education in Madrid.

Don Francisco, who was chosen, was already a friend of ours, and this gave us an interesting window into what went on. When Robert had difficulty in learning Spanish, partly because he spent so much time with his plants and their Latin names, we asked Francisco, at that time head of the boys' school in the village, to help him, and for years he came to tea with Robert every Thursday afternoon. They talked Spanish, became good friends, and Francisco acted as our adviser and informant about many aspects of the local scene. In return Robert was able to give him a lot of information about what had been happening in the outer world during the years of Spain's isolation during and after the Civil War, even several times obtaining from England banned books that had been published in South America about that period.

Francisco's history was interesting. At the outbreak of the Civil War he was a Republican, and as such banned henceforward from teaching in a state school. He managed to live by running a small private school in his home village with considerable struggles. When the war finished, he was re-admitted to the teaching service but sent to an isolated village at the top of a mountain, only accessible on foot or by riding a donkey or horse. Then later he was appointed to our village, where the family added to their income by running the manual telephone exchange. (His daughters helped me with many phone calls in the years before we had a phone: I would write out what I wanted to say and ask them to make my call and tell me the answer.) In the village he was known for his erratic temper, and for drinking too much, presumably partly from frustration, since I don't think there was any sign of either once he got the headship of the new school. He was a very good head, but I think he was perhaps lucky, even then, to be accepted by the administration.

Some of the first shock of making a start was eased by taking in only the three senior *cursos*, that is the children aged eleven to thirteen, for the first month, and then the remainder when the first lot had settled in. All the same it was a formidable task to settle in five hundred children divided into age-groups – horizontally as it were – when previously they had always been divided vertically into small school groups. Things were made worse by the discovery that there were many more children than expected. Someone must have miscounted!

There were of course many difficulties. The arrival of kitchen equipment was delayed, so they could only work in the mornings for some while. When it did arrive the big cooking range could not be got through the doorway and the suppliers' representatives had to be sent for, and, by removing the projecting side pieces and by careful manoeuvring, they were able to ease the monster in.

The children living at a distance were bussed in and stayed to lunch at school, but many of the ones from isolated hamlets were very frightened, and very suspicious indeed of any food with which they were not familiar.

The electrical installation was not complete and for five years there was no telephone. Then there was a serious shortage of specialist teachers for science, art, English and gym, and there was equipment that no one knew how to use. In English, for the first three years, the teaching, such as it was, was given by three successive teachers who had all only had the six-weeks crash course that first summer. Gradually, of course, all these difficulties got sorted out.

However, the Galician country child had two important difficulties. Firstly, at the beginning of their schooling, there was the language. Gallego was, and still is, the language normally spoken in country homes. Like Italian, Portuguese and Castilian (official Spanish), Gallego is derived from Latin, but it is nearer to Portuguese than to Castilian. Until recently all education had, by law, to be in Castilian; thus a six-year-old child starting school and expected to be ready to learn to read had to learn a new language. And as well as the practical aspects of this, there was a psychological one. Galicians have been, in the past, looked down on by other Spaniards as country bumpkins. So a Galician child had, to some extent, to reject the language and culture of his home in order to enter the new world of school.

Now Gallego has a new status. Some years ago Galicia was granted a measure of local autonomy and there has been a great upsurge of patriotism, and, with it, interest in the language and culture of the country. It is now being taught in both primary and secondary schools and an ever-increasing number of books are being published. It is even fashionable among certain classes of intellectuals to speak Gallego, and it is the language of the regional government. And there is Gallego Television, and one of my ex-pupils works for it.

The second difficulty for the country child was the school day at the secondary school in the town. It was a long and tiring day to leave the village on the eight-thirty bus, perhaps after half an hour's walk to get to it, and get back on the seven or eight o'clock bus in the evening. The schools were closed from one p.m. till four p.m., which meant that the children either rushed home for their dinner with just time to get the afternoon bus back, or hung around in Pontevedra, café, park or streets. Some fortunate children had relatives in the town, where they could eat and maybe even do their homework. The bus and the books had to be paid for by the parents. In about 1995, the school day was changed to give a continuous working day from morning till three p.m.

So one way and another, a fair number of children came to me for help with English, from beginners with ambitious parents, strugglers in the summer holidays, to seventeen-year-olds facing the English test in the university entrance exam, and even university students with sometimes very obscure problems. The need gradually lessened. One of my last pupils before I left in 1998 was a young woman preparing for the competitive exam to get into English teaching in a state secondary school. She made it at the third attempt.

As I was leaving Galicia, a whole new reform of education was being implemented, but I had no time then to understand the details. Like so much else, what is so interesting to me is how, in under thirty years, Galician education evolved from the near-medieval to the modern.

23

Changes

"Hoxe todo vai pola nova, si e bon mañan o dira quen poida."
(Gallego saying)
Today everything goes towards the new, if tomorrow is good,
he who can will say.

We watched and lived through so many changes, especially during our
first years in Galicia, as this hidden-away corner of Europe opened up to
influences from outside: from Madrid, the rest of Spain, and from Europe.

Increased prosperity brought modernisation of lifestyles, and
technical advances of every kind, and the conditions of life for the
ordinary country people improved beyond what their grandparents could
even have dreamt of. But inevitably many of the old cultural traditions
are getting forgotten and with them some of the individuality of the
country people gets lost. We were fortunate to have had the opportunity
to catch something of the essence of old Galicia before it was swept
away by progress.

During these years, access to Galicia was transformed. Although
now only cruise ships call in to Vigo and La Coruña with passengers,
the three small airports were enlarged to provided many more flights,
local and international. The Madrid government built big new roads,
and then motorways, thus increasing tourism and opening up the region
to trade with the rest of Spain and Europe, and encouraging industrial
enterprise. Refrigerated lorries now set out every evening from the
fishing ports all up the coast, and drive through the night to take fresh

fish and shellfish to the markets inland. Of course, like everywhere else in Western Europe, the fishing industry has been seriously damaged by the shortage of fish and resulting Common Market quotas.

Locally too, road building brought tarmac lanes to villages and hamlets, and even to individual farms which previously had only been accessible by cart track.

We too got a road. Post-Franco municipal elections gave the district an energetic new mayor, Don Jorge, the highly respected schoolmaster, Lolita's husband. A deeply religious man and a regular churchgoer, it was important to him that there should be a real road to the church, instead of a bumpy track.

Twelve years earlier, there had been a plan to make up the road, but it was necessary to widen the track for one short stretch, and a crusty old bachelor, Don Rosendo, refused to cede a slice of his field unless Don Maximino, the priest, gave him a small triangle of church land which he had long coveted. The priest refused. Everyone got angry and the project was abandoned. The then mayor and Don Maximino were no longer on speaking terms, and no one was friendly with Don Rosendo, who lived in the next parish anyway.

As soon as he could, Don Jorge set about the matter in earnest. He persuaded the priest to write to his superiors for permission to sell the little triangle of land to Don Rosendo, and permission duly came, but the price set by the church authorities (or maybe the priest himself, who had a crop of potatoes growing there) was higher than Don Rosendo would consider.

Stalemate...

Don Jorge did not give up. He went to and fro between the parties and a plan was eventually agreed: the priest would exchange that triangle of land for a piece of Don Rosendo's field beside the church, thus improving the approach, and Don Rosendo would cede the necessary slice of field to the *Ayuntamiento* for the widening of the track. A document was drawn up, but then, at the moment of signing, Don Rosendo refused.

What now? A compulsory purchase order could be obtained but such proceedings are lengthy and Don Jorge was a man of peace. He started negotiating again.

A group of our neighbours who lived along the track then called on Don Jorge and asked, "Don Jorge, suppose that Don Rosendo's wall moved itself back a metre or so during the night?" Don Jorge was sufficiently alarmed by this suggestion to take legal advice, and the lawyer told him what he had already suspected: if that wall moved itself during the night, it would be the *Ayuntamiento's* responsibility to put it back in its place.

A few nights later, Don Rosendo's two big stooks of maize stalks standing in his field burned down. An accident? Certainly not.

Don Jorge decided that the best plan now was to start road-making from both ends, leaving the little stretch in dispute unmade. Maybe Don Rosendo would be shamed into giving way. Work progressed fast and we all went out to watch progress, cheering the workers on. And when only the little stretch in question remained unmade, all of a sudden, Don Rosendo gave way.

In 1975 the National Institute of Statistics made a survey of Spanish houses and published these figures for Galician homes: 29 per cent had no water in the house; 37.7 per cent had only cold water; 41 per cent had no lavatory; 45 per cent used wood for fuel and 49.8 per cent used butane gas. These figures were for both town and country, and obviously there were more amenities in town houses and flats.

From then on, old houses were enlarged or repaired, new houses were built, many in brick and painted brightly in unlikely colours. Kitchens and bathroom, lavatories and septic tanks were installed. More prosperous farms added wrought iron gates to their entrances, possibly painted green or blue, sometimes with the owners' initials picked out in a contrasting colour.

Now most houses have running water, either because their *Ayuntamiento* has provided piped water from a spring on the hill above, or from a storage tank shared by several neighbours, or at least from a tank on the roof holding water pumped up from the well. In the past it was only more prosperous farms, as La Saleta had been, which had their own *mina*. Each farm had its well and some had stone washing tanks. Each village or hamlet had a public washing place, a roofed-over stone tank served by a spring or small stream, with angled flat stones along the front where the clothes were rubbed. It used to be a common sight to see women and girls carrying big tubs of washing on their heads to the washing place which was an important meeting place for friendship, gossip and quarrels.

Celina described the washing process: "The clothes were well soaped and rubbed, then spread out on the grass. You had to keep them damp so you kept sprinkling them all day. Maybe you did it again next day until you were satisfied they were white, and then you rinsed them and laid them out on the grass again to dry. This was before the new detergent powders came in. Now I soak the clothes first and just wash them. But sometimes I wash the sheets by the old method, because if the new powder takes the dirt out so easily, how can it fail to eat up the material?" Now, of course everyone has a washing machine!

When we arrived there were very few tractors. Each family did their own ploughing with their own pair of cows, generally the strong yellow ones.

Now tractors go round from farm to farm, and an increasing number of farmers own their own. A threshing machine now goes round the farms to thresh the rye, a job previously done on each farm's *era* (a stone or concrete platform) by teams of men using a flail consisting of a wooden handle with a wooden club attached to it by leather thongs. The threshers stood in two lines facing each other, and those in each line swung their flails down to pound the rye alternatively and rhythmically. At the end of the day's work they were given a good meal by the farmer. We never saw this, as already when we arrived the machines did the job. Eugenio told me about the first machine which appeared: "It was brought in two parts on two carts. The man who wanted his threshing done sent his cart to fetch either the motor or the machine, and the owner sent his cart over with the other. Then when the job was done and the apparatus moved to the next farm, the family who had finished with it sent one part in their cart, and the next family fetched the other. The big machine which comes now is a great improvement." The rye is cut in June and threshed in July or August. And we used to hear the machine's noisy progress round the neighbourhood as it approached, going from farm to farm, throwing up clouds of dust.

Wages have more than doubled and prices too. People dress and eat better. Cinemas and dance halls flourish. *Fiestas* are bigger and noisier and more sophisticated, with two bands to play alternately, and, much more expensive. The motor car has transformed the life of the people, and in some household budgets a car comes higher in the list of aspirations than a bathroom, and much higher than any domestic gadgets such as washing machines.

With improved standards of living and raised expectations, something of the old co-operation between neighbours has been lost, and a sense of civic responsibility is slow to grow in its place. Ernesto told me that it is now difficult to obtain the neighbours' help for such jobs as repairing a track way, in spite of the fact that more of them own cars and therefore have a personal interest in its condition. They feel that "they" – the *Ayuntamiento* or the government – should repair the track.

Nevertheless, standards of living were still below those of the other countries of Western Europe, except Portugal. The young people, in particular, felt the lack of opportunities. Since the death of Franco, demonstrations and strikes have been permitted, and in the towns there have been plenty of both, serving as an outlet for much bottled-up discontent. But in the country, who can you protest to, with any chance of being listened to?

Free municipal elections in 1979 swept away some old abuses together with the old mayor and village council. The new mayor, Don Jorge, was elected mainly because of his known integrity; the *Ayuntamiento* has a paid secretary, honest and hardworking, and in our village at least, local democracy works well.

There are still vestiges of the old *caciquismo,* slow to disappear. *Caciques* were village bosses who, because of their political or economic position, held power over the other people of the district. The word is derived from an American-Indian word meaning "chief". Many years ago, we were told of such a gentleman in a village nearby. He had friends in high places, and when these needed their vines pruned, for example, he would order a group of men to go and do the work. They received no pay, though probably a good lunch, but they would have been very unwise to refuse to go. Next time a permit was required from the *Ayuntamiento,* or there was a dispute with a neighbour, or a new road was to be made near their land.... Old habits die hard and such practices take time to disappear, not least because many countrymen expected to be treated in this way.

Change was already under way with Spain's recovery after the Civil War, but the real catalyst was Franco's death in 1975. It so happened that we were away for several months during that time, so we missed the opportunity to observe the immediate local reactions to such a major event.

When we returned the first and most obvious change was that the newspapers began to comment openly on political issues. Previously there had been covert comment for those who understood the delicate art of reading between the lines, and who knew how to judge more by what was not said than by what was said. Our friend Don Francisco was highly skilled at this. In shops and bars, conversations no longer dried up when a stranger entered and our friends began to tell us their opinions. There was a real fear though of awakening dormant passions, of touching old wounds, because of the terrible years of Civil War. People tended to express a certain fatalistic pessimism, perhaps not always genuine, as if they were afraid to seem naïve if they allowed their hopes for a new era to be obvious, or perhaps because they did not believe that anything could change very much. Fear of violence and genuine pessimism there certainly were. Spain has been badly governed for many centuries, and abuses of power have been a normal part of the life of the country, not least in Franco's time. Corruption, non-payment of taxes, *caciquismo*, a cumbersome bureaucracy, *enchufismo* (literally "being plugged in", that is having friends in high places who can recommend you for jobs et cetera), these things take time to sweep away. They will not be swept away unless sufficient people believe that it can be done and are prepared to co-operate in the work of doing so. Over the succeeding years confidence has grown, and successive governments have tackled these issues with reasonable on-going success.

On 15th June 1977, there was the first general election for forty-one years. There had been elections in Franco's time in which one fifth of the members of the *Cortes* (Parliament) were directly elected by the "heads of families" of the country, but their votes scarcely affected the issue, since there were no political parties except General Franco's and therefore no opposition. Thus, in effect, no one under sixty-four had voted in a free election. To us this was an astonishing thought. Understandably, the country people had very little idea what the election was about, and until the last moment many of them were undecided who to vote for, or how to vote, or even whether to vote at all.

Their problem was made worse by the complicated system of proportional representation adopted, and by the huge number of political parties. As well as the national parties, in Galicia there were several regional parties, who, in spite of meetings and negotiations, failed to agree to amalgamate or even to join loosely together in groups. The television ran a number of programmes attempting to explain but not much was understood.

In the towns there was a great build-up of excitement. For weeks before the event, Pontevedra was awash with leaflets just thrown around in the streets, and loud-speaker vans drove slowly round and round, blaring out their messages. Notice boards were provided for posters, but many were then torn down, presumably by rival factions. A friend of ours who was in Madrid during the week before the election told us that we had seen nothing. Madrid had been in a wild state of excitement, strain and acute nervousness.

In the village, anxiety increased as the day drew near. They were being asked to vote, but who for and what would be the outcome? Families waited for "Father" to decide.

The day of the election when María-Ester came with the milk, I asked her if she was all set to go down to the village to vote.

"Oh, I've not thought about it," she said. I said that it was an obligation.

"Oh, is it *obligatorio* [compulsory]?"

"No," I said, "but the Gallegos have been complaining for centuries that no one in Madrid pays any attention to them and their problems. Now you are being asked your opinion. If you don't go and vote, what right have you to complain in the future?"

"I must talk about it at home," she said. And next day she told me that she and Eugenio had voted.

In the past, elections were notoriously rigged, and this time, the provisional government drew up careful rules of procedure to try to avoid even the suspicion of corruption. The voting was by parishes; each parish had its electoral table, presided over by a president and two assistants, who were the most educated persons in the parish. Each political party had the right to send an observer to watch the proceedings. In each electoral district the political parties had got out printed lists of their candidates for the *Cortes* and the elector had to choose the list he favoured, and put it in the envelope provided, which he then posted in the ballot box. For the Senate, there was one single list for the whole province, printed on pink paper, and the elector had to put crosses by the names of the three candidates of his choice, put it in a pink envelope and post it in a different ballot box. There were booths provided for those who desired privacy, and no one who was not a voter was allowed to enter the polling station – not even the Civil Guard. This meant that we could not go and watch.

The president of the electoral table had to be a person with a university degree, if there was such a person living in the parish. In our parish the only one was a son of the doctor, who had graduated the previous year in Agriculture. He was assisted by the manager of the Savings Bank branch, and the son of the clerk of the *Ayuntamiento*, who had some technical qualification. When the poll closed, each parish team had to count their votes and the representatives of the political parties had the right to stay to watch this done. The results then had to be phoned or telegraphed in to the district centre, who correlated the figures for the area and then telegraphed these to Madrid.

The results came in slowly, very slowly. The various electoral tables had no experience of counting and checking and the tellers in each district had no experience either. There were many isolated parishes, some with no telephone or telegraph office. Switchboards jammed and telegrams travelled slowly.

The following days the newspapers carried many funny stories, as well as accounts of real difficulties. One old lady arrived at a polling station in Galicia and asked the president to fill in her paper for her because "there are a whole crowd of names here and I don't know any of them". The president had to refuse, of course, and after some thought, the old lady announced that she would vote for the "President's men". Another old lady arrived shouting that she wanted to be shown where and how to vote for Franco. She produced a newspaper photo of him which she wanted to put in the envelope for the Senate. In another polling station a man arrived with the completed voting slips for his twenty employees, and was quite put out when it was explained to him that he could not do that. Why not, he said, since he had always done this in the past?

By and large it seems that the election was fairly conducted. The big majority for the acting President, *Señor* Suarez's centre group, was perhaps unduly weighted by the number of undecided and uninformed country people who, like the old lady, wanted to vote for the President "because he seems a good chap". The big surprise was the small number of votes polled by *Alianza Popular*, the right-wing party of old Francoists and ultra-conservatives. Evidently the country was quite sure that it wanted a change.

Since that first election many years have passed and democracy has established itself. At first fear of Communism went very deep, and anyway some people were afraid of any change that might affect their personal (and especially financial) well-being. Others were fundamentally cynical about the morality of governments. But all enjoyed their new freedom to criticise.

24

Eugenio and Celina

"Tras de tempo, tempo." (Gallego saying)
After time, time comes.

One event we never expected: shortly after María-Ester's wedding, as now she and her husband could look after the farm, Eugenio and Celina flew to Brazil to visit their two sons who had paid for the trip. It was a most remarkable experience for them! First there was the journey in the plane. "How comfortable it was," said Celina. "It must be much more comfortable to travel by air than in a ship!" Before they left they had come to us for advice about the journey.

"Don Roberto," said Eugenio, "I want to take some money to spend in Brazil and how do I carry it? Can I carry pesetas in my pocket? Can we take some bottles of *aguardiente* for our sons, and some of our own salt pork?"

They were very impressed by San Paulo with its skyscrapers, huge long beach and rich suburbs. "Lots of houses like yours," Eugenio told us, "but some terribly poor people too, especially the Indians. They live in sort of shacks. I have never seen anyone so poor in Spain." Their sons were doing well, each of them owning a bar and a grocery shop, "Like a supermarket – much bigger than Lolita's shop – and they both own cars and drive very fast. The grandchildren are not so well brought up as children here in Galicia, but they are doing well at school."

The food? Well, there was poor quality fish, but good meat and strange vegetables and herbs. Eugenio had not liked it at all, and only ate out of tins, but Celina had enjoyed the strange tastes and spices, and had put on a lot of weight.

"Yes, we are glad to be back at home," they said, "but how wonderful it was!"

★

In September 1986 a very tragic event occurred. One morning very early, Eugenio got up from his bed, which he shared with his small grandson, went down to the *alpendre* and hanged himself from a beam. He used a new rope, which he had bought the previous day, perhaps for the purpose.

No one knew or knows why. He had confided in no one, and had no urgent financial or social problems. There had been a period of unhappy family relationships because he had quarrelled with his son-in-law, María-Ester's husband, and as a result the young couple and their children had gone to live a few kilometres away, but those difficulties had been sorted out and the young couple had returned to live at the farm. All seemed to be going well.

Eugenio did suffer from gout and the doctor had warned him not to drink much red wine, and he found this a hardship. He had also had a hernia for years which gave him considerable pain at times. He refused to have an operation because he was terrified of doctors, hospitals, and even injections. Was his hernia particularly painful that night?

He was afraid of old age, I think. He was sixty-five when he died, just one year older than me, and we had often joked about growing old. Maybe his gloomy prognostications about the infirmities of old age were more deeply felt than I had realised. On the other hand he was very fatalistic. Once when I gave him a lift in the car to Pontevedra, I insisted that he should fasten his seat belt. "Doña Margarita," he said, "I believe that the *Señor* in Heaven has a book, and if it is written down in His book that Doña Margarita and Eugenio will die this Friday, in an accident on the road to Pontevedra, then that is what will happen. It won't make any difference at all whether we have fastened our seat belts."

It was a horrible disaster for his family. María-Ester took over the farm with the help of her husband at weekends. Celina fell and broke her leg, and then gradually slid downhill into premature senility.

We missed Eugenio very much. We owed so much to his friendship and that of his family. Besides welcoming us on a human basis as people, he interpreted our behaviour to the other villagers and explained their ways to us. So too did Lolita and many other people in various walks of life. To all of them, very many thanks.

Part Four

The Garden

25

A plantsman's garden

"What exactly is a plantsman?" (Nigel Colborn: article in *The Garden*, RHS, June 2003)

I think that Robert was a plantsman. However, there are some other questions which have no definitive answers, or which have many answers. What is a garden? What is a garden for? What is a botanical garden?

In 1975 we visited Australia. Robert went by sea and so was able to visit La Orotava (Tenerife), Kirstenbosch (Cape Town) and the Botanical gardens of Perth, Canberra, Sydney and Melbourne. He had already a number of South African and Australian plants growing at La Saleta, but now he was delighted to see the enormous variety there were, and returned to Galicia with even greater enthusiasm.

To make room for more "Australians", he had the vegetable garden moved to the bottom of the field down the north side of the *finca*. There probably the soil was richer, and we had never had enough manure for them on the higher slope because, as Ernesto kept pointing out, we lacked a cow. Raspberries, strawberries and fruit trees, apples, greengages and plums were happy in their new position, but the vegetables got neglected and then forgotten. I confess I found it easier and cheaper to buy them in the market!

So now the whole middle area down that side turned into what became justly known as the "Australian jungle". And as he propagated yet more interesting "Australians", he established a further, lesser

Australian jungle along the north boundary of the bottom field. In retrospect, I think it was at this time that he began to lose sight of the design aspect in his excitement with all these melaleucas, callistemons, acacias, grevilleas and hakeas, et cetera.

He planted a collection of "South Africans" along the terraces below the chapel, including a number of different species of protea, but, after a beautiful start, sadly they proved delicate and few survived more than a few years. Many others did well, however: *Brabejum stellatifolium*, *Dais cotinifolia*, and aloes, gazanias and lampranthus, mesembrianthemum, watsonias, and agapanthus. English narcissi failed and the mice ate the crocus bulbs.

Immediately below the house, formal rose beds surrounded the lily pond with its goldfish and abundance of noisy frogs. The roses flowered magnificently but the plants were never robust and proved short-lived, probably because they flowered from April till November so had an insufficient rest period.

The rhododendrons, planted in 1970 in the shade of the oak wood, did very well indeed, and they and the roses were the only plants which had to be regularly watered in summer, or rather that Robert would water, since his policy overall was that his plants, once established, should grow or not grow in the existing conditions, part of the research aspect of garden making.

Magnolias were very successful as, of course, were camellias which had been flourishing in Galicia for many years. Robert's collection grew and grew as he added a group of *C X williamsii* hybrids and *C X reticulata* and *reticulata* hybrids from the well-known japonicas, and a small collection of other species of camellia, many of which were newly discovered by plant hunters.

There was an annual Camellia Show in Galicia, rotating between Vigo, Pontevedra, and Villagarcía. This was the social event of the spring and there was great competition for prizes. Neither Robert nor I had presentation skills, but in later years he twice won the big prize, the Gold Camellia, for a collection of species, some of which had hardly been known until then. He also wrote several monographs about camellias for such occasions.

The study of camellias became more and more important to him as he added to his collection and researched the history of their introduction into Europe, and specifically their introduction into Spain and Portugal, and followed the ever-growing number of new hybrids being produced in Australia, New Zealand, the USA, and Great Britain. During our winter visits to London, he spent many hours in the RHS Lindley Library, and made an album of illustrations from the books he found there. He also made a contribution, on those established in Spain and Portugal, to the International Camellia Society's Camellia Register.

A highlight indeed was the visit of the International Camellia Society to Galicia in 1981. It was a big group, a coach load of Australians, one of New Zealanders, another of French, and another of English, 140 people in all. We were not directly involved in the detailed organisation though Robert's advice was sought and valued, and we played a big part in helping entertain and inform the visitors. They visited seven or eight gardens including La Saleta and were interested in the contrast between the *pazo* gardens and our new, half-made one.

A variety of things went wrong, mainly to do with timetables and coaches. The English and French parties had local coaches and drivers and even they did not know the way to some of these private gardens, but the Australian and New Zealand coaches had driven up from Madrid with Madrid drivers and these kept getting lost in the Galician lanes. After the first day, those of us who knew the gardens divided ourselves between the groups, and I rode about in the New Zealand coach. The driver was awkward, and the Italian-born lady guide knew nothing about local matters, and did not get on with the driver at all. I was pushed to the front, given the microphone and told: "Now please tell us about Galicia" – and, unspoken, "keep the peace".

The visit ended with a banquet in the San Francisco monastery in Santiago de Compostela, and a group of minstrels in traditional costume appeared, as dinner finished, playing guitars and singing as they mingled among the guests. A splendid occasion.

In January 1983 we had a visit of a group of botanists and their wives, one of whom, Santiago Castroviejo, was the then Director of the *Real Jardín Botánico de Madrid*. He took Robert aside and made a suggestion: they wanted to set up a national botanic garden outside Madrid, and thought La Saleta might be just the place. What would we think about such an idea? We thought it a fantasy but that he was putting out a feeler. So we considered it seriously. Nothing more was said on that occasion and they left promising to send seeds to Robert to try out.

The next time he came, the idea had developed somewhat. Suppose we sold them the main part of the garden while keeping for ourselves the new house and its immediate surroundings? Robert suggested working out the price on the basis of the value of local agricultural land, and I thought that perhaps Santiago was expecting a bigger element of gift. In this way we would ensure the future of the garden. We had noticed on a number of occasions that some Spaniards over-estimated our wealth because so many of the garden-owners in Galicia had more than one home, and so they supposed that we had a home in England.

We consulted our children, and also got in touch with the English National Trust to find out what sort of agreements were made in such cases and what sort of difficulties might arise. Some months later, Santiago wrote that he had approached the Madrid Ministry of Culture who said they had no money for such a scheme.

In 1985 Santiago brought a senior administrator from the Ministry of Culture, Uxia Labarta of the Department of Scientific Research, to see the situation and the garden. Over lunch, the latter went straight to the point. First he asked practical questions: what would it cost to run the garden and how many gardeners would be needed? We had one and a half gardeners – one full-time and one half-time. Obviously more were needed.

Then he explained that his department was in a difficult position because, though they had money to start up projects, they were very short of money to run them, with the result that none of their projects was working well for lack of adequate staff. So they could do nothing just now. So the matter rested there, and years later, when I asked Robert if he thought anything would ever come of the idea, he said yes, he thought so, but for now it was ahead of its time. Spain was very busy with modernisation, of roads, schools, universities, hospitals and the forestry and fishing industries, so gardens were a very low priority.

There were other groups who came during these years; those that I remember were from the International Dendrological Society, the Royal Horticultural Society, and an American group. Also many individuals came, of whom the most unforgettable was a Japanese professor, an expert on camellias. This gentleman, personally charming and very interesting, slept only four hours a night, smoked eighty cigarettes a day, and spoke a mixed language he called "European". He had such vitality that Robert and I were exhausted by the end of week he stayed with us. The two camellia enthusiasts visited the gardens around, discussed camellias, dissected camellias, classified camellias and photographed them and their detailed parts. Meanwhile I kept the household going, cooked big pots of rice because "Japanese stomach very small", and tried to prevent draughts of air, or the cat, from disturbing any of the exhibits arranged all over the hall and sitting room floor, awaiting attention and photography.

In the summer of 1984 the well-known botanist, Antonio López Lillo, visited us for the first time and then became a valued friend. Years later he wrote of his first visit to La Saleta, in *Zona Verde*, the bulletin of the Spanish Association of Public Parks and Gardens, winter 1993: (I translate) "I can say that observing such a big collection (of plants) surprised me, not only on account of their number, but on account of the rarity of most of the species. It was much more than I had imagined, I thought I was seeing the best private botanic garden in Spain. There were more than a thousand species, very varied, many new to me, many of them the only examples in Spain and some, almost certainly, the only examples in Europe."

By 1987 many of Robert's shrubs and trees had grown big and beautiful, and the whole was taking shape. However, in a practical sense, the garden was unfinished. There is an enormous amount of work involved in making a new garden of this size and more time, more money and more gardeners were needed to complete the task. It seems to me that Robert's real achievement was as a plantsman and innovator. His answer to "What is a garden for?" would have been: "A suitable area in which to plant interesting, unusual and beautiful plants and observe their progress, success or failure." Anyway, finished or unfinished, the La Saleta garden was beautiful, and he had given great pleasure to many people and fulfilled a large part of his dream.

In the autumn of 1987 we went to England for a visit, and it was there that Robert died suddenly and unexpectedly. His great adventure was over.

Epilogue

Obviously there were difficulties: sometimes we were frustrated, annoyed, lonely. There were language and culture barriers that had to be surmounted as best we could. Individuals have been unfriendly, unhelpful or have thought they could take advantage of us, as is it to be expected anywhere in the world. But they have been very few.

Of course we were in a very privileged position, on the one hand because of the importance of the La Saleta *finca*, especially the chapel, to the village. And on the personal level because we could and did go to England every year, and our family and friends came to stay, so that we never felt exiled.

Our project "Go to Galicia" arose in our lives at a time when we were both ready for it. As the children had been growing up and leaving home, I had embarked on an ambitious project of my own which proved excessively difficult because Robert had found himself incapable of wholeheartedly supporting me with it, partly because, just at this time, a crisis occurred in his business – a family firm facing collapse, and eventually bought out by a larger one, as had happened to so many in that period.

So, he dreaming of making a garden, and I very attracted by the Galician world, language and culture, both of us were ready for a new adventure, and both of us, fully co-operating, were necessary to plan it, embark on it and carry it out to a good level of success. It is a richness to have two countries and we were fortunate to have the opportunity. It gave us a freshness of the senses and a freshness of spirit, an understanding and acceptance of differentness.

The life of the village has gone on changing and moving into the modern world – gains and losses. The village world we found in 1970 is now part of history, and we too played a small part in its history.

Postscript

In 1987 we were in England for a winter visit when Robert died suddenly. He was seventy-six years old and I was ten years younger. As soon as I could, I went back to La Saleta to be greeted by our gardeners, Ernesto and Julio, with great warmth. It was as if they had feared that I would not come back.

How would I cope? Could I manage the administration of the property, carry on developing the garden, control the men, make ends meet? Alone?

In our absence, the 1987 gale, which did so much damage in France and England, had swept in from the Atlantic, and across the north of Spain on its way, and although the men had done a lot of clearing up there was plenty more to do.

I felt that La Saleta was my home, and I was thankful to find that, yes, I could sleep at night. All new widows have a great many problems, as well as the normal grief and shock, personal, administrative and financial, although having too much to do may have a steadying effect.

Neighbouring friends called to offer condolences, and one of my sons was able to come for Christmas to help me. We spent Christmas Day with young friends, climbing Monte Pindo near Finisterre and having a picnic on the top. Life goes on.

Gradually, with total loyalty and co-operation from Ernesto and Julio, the garden was got into better order. Gradually, I learnt more about the plants from visiting botanists and horticulturists, especially Antonio López Lillo, who showed me how to identify them from the reference books. The Madrid Botanic Garden sent a team who stayed several days, helping me and taking cuttings and baby plants to try out in Madrid. The second winter, a young Canadian woman, who had just finished her training at Kew Gardens, came for a working holiday and taught us how to prune shrubs. Ernesto commented, "Don Roberto would not allow you to do that," and I could only answer, "But we haven't got Don Roberto!"

A grant from the Regional Government helped me with running expenses for several years, and when that came to an end, I was able to cut and sell the mature pines from the woodland for a good price, and then had the area replanted with chestnuts, with the help of another grant, available for reforestation with native trees.

So the years went by, and they were busy years. A new branch of the village electricity line came near enough that, after long drawn-out negotiations, I managed to get us connected to it, and so could get rid of our private line and transformer which had been struck by lightning several times and needed expensive repairs each time. Later, the swimming pool leaked and had to be remade, as did the lily pond.

We needed more gardeners but wages were rising, rightly, and the cost of living too. Several summers I had some student help, and then a friend made a brilliant suggestion. We had been letting the old house to English holidaymakers for years, and he suggested that we let it, out of season, free in exchange for so many hours of work per week in the garden. There were not a lot of takers for this work option, but it was very rewarding and led to friendships that have lasted to this day. One married couple came four years running.

Yes, I was sometimes lonely. I continued to give English lessons, both in Pontevedra and in the village and thus made new contacts. The friends that Robert and I had already made, kept in close touch, and told me to invite myself to lunch or for a weekend when I wanted, which I did, and was most grateful.

I continued to celebrate the fiesta each year, Mass in the chapel and lunch in the house. I needed someone suitable to preside at the other end of the long table, and the new priest agreed to do so, and brought his wine for the occasion each year. Family and friends came for holidays, tenants came to the old house, and visiting groups came from time to time to see the garden. So I had plenty of good human contacts. During the last year or two before I left, I was even opening the garden for visitors on Saturday afternoons. Very many heartfelt thanks to all those people who helped me in so many different ways.

From the beginning, it was obvious that, sooner or later, I would have to sell and return to England to live. Apart from rising costs, La Saleta was not a suitable place to live alone into real old age. Selling proved difficult.

At first I hoped to find an organisation that would carry on and develop the garden further. The Madrid Botanic Garden tried but failed to find the money, and I could not afford to give the property away. It was my only home. I tried contacting other organisations with the same answer: "No money." This was the time when Galicia was modernising rapidly, improving roads, schools and medical care. In reality the whole project was ten years ahead of its time.

Next, I thought about possibly finding another foreigner and advertised in gardening magazines in England, France, Belgium, and then in Madrid newspapers, and local ones. Over the years a trickle of possible buyers wrote for details or came to see, even one or two probable drug dealers, hoping to launder their money. Luckily, I never had to directly refuse one of these, and there was no chance that the property could be bought for development. But, in truth, it was too big and too good for its environment.

So I came to the conclusion that the most sensible solution was to divide it, which led to a difficulty with the Regional Government, because it had been listed for protection as a *pazo*. However, I appealed on the grounds that it had never been more than a big farm, and that Severo Perez had had ideas above his social station when he built his chapel. A team of young architects was sent, who agreed with me, and only the old buildings and area around them remained protected.

So, in the end, I divided the property into four parts and sold them, one by one, to four different owners, the final piece, the new house and its surroundings in March 1998. I had been alone at La Saleta for eleven years.

I packed up, sent my furniture to England, said my goodbyes and, in June, drove away in my overloaded car into torrents of rain, with the tears pouring down my cheeks.

Glossary

Of Spanish and Gallego words, as used in the text

Aduana	customs
Aguardiente	spirit distilled from pips and skins of grapes
Albariño	the best of the Galician wines
Alcalde	Mayor of municipal district
Alpendre	open-sided farmyard shed
Aparejador	quantity surveyor
Asilo	old people's home
Ayuntamiento	municipal government in general; building used
Bacalao	salt dried cod
Bachillerato	school-leaving exam
Bicho	insect or animal (pejorative)
Bodega	wine cellar
Burra	female donkey
Cacique	local boss, often political
Caciquismo	system of local bosses
Caldo gallego	soup-stew made of salt pork, potatoes and turnip tops
Callos	tripe; dish made of tripe and other ingredients
Caramba!	Good gracious!
Carballo (gallego)	oak tree
Carnaval	the fiesta held before Lent begins
Casa	house
Casero	caretaker
Catalán	(here) a kind of grape, kind of wine
Centolla	spider crab

Chorizo	hard pork sausage, eaten raw, like salami
Churros	little fingers of fried batter
Concentración	(here) re-allocation of fields to concentrate holdings
Consejo	municipal council
Cristóbal	Christopher
Curso	course, each year's work in school or college
Depósito	store, warehouse, pound
Dios	God
Doñ, Doña	titles of respect used with the Christian name
EGB	*Educacion General Básica;* primary education up to fourteen
Empanada	pie made of fish or meat in bread dough or pastry
Empanadilla	small individual pie
Enchufe	a power plug. Fig. To have friends in high places
Enchufismo	the system of *enchufes*
Entierro	funeral
Era	threshing floor; now used to mean farmyard
Faro de Vigo	the Vigo daily newspaper
Finca	a piece of land, with or without a house, property
Funeral	memorial service
Gallego	adjective; the language of Galicia; a native of Galicia
Gaseosa	cheapest from of lemonade
Gestoría	agency acting as intermediary between government and citizen
Guardia Civil	Civil guard, i.e. police
Hermandad	
Syndical	State-sponsored trade union
Hórreo	small grain store on stilts
Industrias	something like our Factory Inspectorate
Juez de la Paz	local Justice of the Peace
Lareira (gallego)	open stone shelf for the cooking fire in old kitchens
Lugar	place; hamlet
Madrina	godmother
Mañana	tomorrow, morning
Mejora	improvement – use in Galicia explained in text
Membrillo	quince pate

Mina	(here) underground water channel for water from spring
Minifundia	tiny plots of land
Monaguillo	Lit: little monk – the boy who helps the priest
Monte	uncultivated hillside or woodland
Novio (fem: novia)	sweetheart, fiancé
Padrinos	godparents
Palmero	pilgrim carrying palm leaves, palmer
Pazo	Galician manor house
Peregrino	pilgrim
Permiso	permit
Pipa	522 litres of wine: the barrel that holds that amount
Pólizas	government stamps to be affixed to documents. et cetera
Pozo	well
Practicante	doctor's assistant. He gives injections, et cetera.
Queimada (gallego)	brew made by burning *aguardiente* and adding sugar.
Rato (gallego)	mouse (in Castilian Spanish, a mouse = *raton)*
Rata (gallego)	female mouse (in Castilian Spanish = rat)
Residencia	residence; residence permit
Ría	arm of the sea, like a Norwegian fjord
Romería	religious celebration and open-air fiesta at some holy place such as a hill-top shrine, chapel et cetera.
Real Jardín Botánico	Royal Botanic Garden
Santo (fem. Santa)	saint. There is also the abbreviated form *San*
Señor, Señora	Mr, Mrs
Serafín	Seraphin
Sí	yes
Sobrina	niece
Tornaratos	Mushroom-shaped stones to keep mice from climbing into the *hórreo.*
Turrón	nutty toffee
Vale	OK
Viuda	widow

Bibliography

In English

Epton, Nina, *Grapes and Granite*, 1956
  Spain's Magic Coast
Gadow, Hans, *In Northern Spain*, Black, London, 1897
Hell, Vera and Hellmut, *The Great Pilgrimage of the Middle Ages*, Barrie & Rockliff, 1964
Meakin, Annette M B, *Galicia, the Switzerland of Spain*, Methuen, London, 1909
Wigram, Edward, *Northern Spain*, Black, 1906

Novels in English

Yglesias, José, *The Goodbye Land*, Hutchinson, London, 1968
Pardo Bazán, Emilia, *The House of Ulloa* (English translation, See below, Penguin Classics 1990)

In Spanish

Castroviejo, José María, *Galicia, Guia Espiritual de una Tierra*, Espasa Calpe, 1960
Losada, Basilio, *Galicia*, Editorial Taber, 1969
Otero Pedrayo, Ramón, *Guia de Galicia*, Galaxia, Vigo
Fariño Jamardo, José, *La Parroquia Rural en Galicia*, Madrid, 1975
Lisón Tolesana, Carmelo, *Antropología Cultural de Galicia*, Madrid, 1971
Risco, Vicente, *Historia de Galicia, Galaxia*, Vigo, 1952
Rodriguez López, Jesús, *Supersticiones de Galicia,* first published 1895

Novels

Fernández Florez, Wenceslao, *Volvereta, El Bosque Animado*
García Sanchez, José, *Mi Aldea*, Toledo, 1927
Lueiro Rey, Manuel, *Manso*, first published in Madrid 1967
Pardo Bazán, Emilia, *Los Pazos de Ulloa*, first published 1886, see above.
    La Madre Naturaleza, 1887
Quiroga, Elena, *Viento del Norte, La Enferma*, 1955
Valle-Inclan, Ramón del, some of his many novels and short stories
Rivas, Manuel, *El Lápiz del Carpintero*, 1998, Alfaguara
Ozores Marchesi, Javier, *La Cena de los Videntes*, Arenas 2001

In Gallego

Castalao, Alfonso R, *As Cruces de Pedra na Galiza*, first published 1950.
New edition Akal Editor, Madrid 1975. This is a beautifully illustrated
    book with a summary in English.
Zamora Mosquera, Federico, *Refráns e Ditos Populares Galegos*, Galaxia
    1972

General Books about Modern Spain

John Hooper, *The New Spaniards*, Penguin Books, 2nd edition, 2006
Giles Tremlett, *Ghosts of Spain*, Faber and Faber, 2006
Paul Preston, *The Triumph of Democracy in Spain*, Methuen & Co, 1986
Jason Webster, *Guerra!*, Transworld Publishers, 2006